T0009482

KINGDOM
VALUES
Devotional

Books by Tony Evans

Kingdom Men
Kingdom Men Rising Devotional
Kingdom Values

KINGDOM VALUES

Devotional

TONY EVANS

BETHANYHOUSE

a division of Baker Publishing Group
Minneapolis, Minnesota

© 2023 by Tony Evans

Published by Bethany House Publishers
Minneapolis, Minnesota
www.bethanyhouse.com

Bethany House Publishers is a division of
Baker Publishing Group, Grand Rapids, Michigan

Printed in the United States of America

Library of Congress Cataloging-in-Publication Data
Names: Evans, Tony, author. | Evans, Tony, Kingdom values.
Title: Kingdom values devotional / Tony Evans.
Description: Minneapolis, Minnesota : Bethany House Publishers, a division of Baker Publishing Group, [2023] | Includes bibliographical references.
Identifiers: LCCN 2023002689 | ISBN 9780764241895 (cloth) | ISBN 9781493443871 (ebook)
Subjects: LCSH: Character—Religious aspects—Christianity. | Christians—Prayers and devotions.
Classification: LCC BV4599.5.C45 E933 2023 | DDC 241/.4—dc23/eng/20230324
LC record available at https://lccn.loc.gov/2023002689

Cover design by Dan Pitts

Baker Publishing Group publications use paper produced from sustainable forestry practices and post-consumer waste whenever possible.

23   24   25   26   27   28   29   7   6   5   4   3   2   1

KINGDOM VALUES
INTRODUCTION

We live in a time of cultural chaos. One of the primary reasons for this is the absence and rejection of a commonly held values system that develops and transfers a righteous and justice standard for character development based on an objective standard of truth.

Values refer to the desirable qualities that build character in people's lives. When the right values in the lives of people are cancelled or replaced by the wrong values, then not only is the character of a person diminished, but the environment in which they live becomes increasingly chaotic.

There is a need for God's people to lead the way in communicating and modeling God's values system in their own lives, and then aggressively transferring biblical values to those within the sphere of their influence.

God has given us a clearly defined list of values that ought to be the pursuit of everyone who takes God and His Word seriously. Because God and His Word are truth, then the values He outlines for us in the Beatitudes provide us the perfect paradigm for helping to replace chaos in the culture with order, decency, honesty, purity, unity, spirituality, and a myriad of other benefits that can help bring order to an otherwise uncivil life and society.

When God's truth serves as the foundation for defining and identifying the building blocks of character as His values are developed in and through our lives, then we can begin to see and experience the blessing and divine favor that He promises as the natural outgrowth, outcome, and result of operating on a kingdom values system.

Each devotional in this book provides a Scripture passage, a reflection, a chance for you to react and reflect on what you've read, and a prayer. Our hope is that these daily readings will help you think through God's truth and then apply it to your life. The end goal is for you to reflect the character and values of God in your family, your church, and your community.

One

"But when He, the Spirit of truth, comes, He will guide you into all the truth; for He will not speak on His own initiative, but whatever He hears, He will speak; and He will disclose to you what is to come."

John 16:13

Truth reigns as the fundamental building block upon which all else either stands tall or topples. Somehow our culture has made followers of truth look like second-class citizens, outdated or old-fashioned. It's popular to believe truth is subjective, or that everyone should search out "their own truth." But truth, it turns out, is universal—we can't make it up as we go along. Truth be told, everyone depends on truth.

Without truth, the whole world will collapse. Even the opponents of truth depend on it to function every day.

For example, how would you feel about flying on an airplane with an unsure pilot? If you heard your pilot come on the speaker before the flight and say, "We are about to take off and I'm pretty sure I know what buttons to push, but sometimes I like to mix it up," what would you do? If you were like me, you would get off that plane.

Or, how would you feel about a surgeon who has discarded truth in his or her field? Let's say you were having a consultation with a surgeon and he or she said, "I watched a surgery like this online the other day and that surgeon was doing some pretty cool new things that I'd like to try to save time. I think I know where to cut, but I'll look again at that video just to be sure." Would you even stay for the rest of the consultation or would you, like me, get up and walk away?

What about a pharmacist who admits to guessing as your medication is put in the bottle? Would you take it? Or what if the pharmacist said, "I have a lot of meds to choose from on these shelves. Let me pick one that I feel is right for you!"

Truth governs all we rely on for our very existence. The truth that makes up the oxygen we breathe or the gravity that keeps us on this earth can't vary based on how it feels. We need truth, more than we realize sometimes.

Reaction: On a scale of 1 to 10 (with 10 being the most), indicate how highly you esteem truth as an absolute standard we must all follow.

1---2---3---4---5---6---7---8---9---10

On a scale of 1 to 10 (with 10 being the most), indicate how highly you feel our society esteems truth as an absolute standard we must all follow.

1---2---3---4---5---6---7---8---9---10

What do you think is the major reason for the difference between the two scores?

Prayer: *Jesus, guide me into the full knowledge of truth. Show me where I am in error in my thoughts or beliefs so that I can correctly align myself under Your truth. Help our society to value truth more fully and honor it through actions that glorify You. Reveal ways in which I can better influence society and those around me to both love and value truth. Thank You for all You are doing in this area in my life. In Your name, amen.*

Two

> But realize this, that in the last days difficult times will come. For men will be lovers of self, lovers of money, boastful, arrogant, revilers, disobedient to parents, ungrateful, unholy, unloving, irreconcilable, malicious gossips, without self-control, brutal, haters of good, treacherous, reckless, conceited, lovers of pleasure rather than lovers of God, holding to a form of godliness, although they have denied its power; Avoid such men as these. For among them are those who enter into households and captivate weak women weighed down with sins, led on by various impulses, always learning and never able to come to the knowledge of the truth.
>
> 2 Timothy 3:1–7

Have you ever played hide-and-seek? If you have, then you know that while one person counts, the rest of the people playing go hide. Well, it seems that in today's culture, truth has gone and hid. It's not hidden because God has hidden it. No, it's been hidden by the overabundance of our reliance on our emotions and ideologies to guide our thoughts and beliefs.

Too much of our culture today is operating based on how they want to think. Like the verse in Judges,

"In those days there was no king in Israel; everyone did what was right in his own eyes" (21:25).

Decisions these days are primarily being made based on feelings. Truth is being redefined based on feelings. Cultural norms are being established based on feelings. And while that is dangerous in and of itself, it gets even more dangerous when you realize that feelings change. In fact, they can change on a dime. Not only that, but feelings are different based on who you are and what perspective you have.

Feelings don't determine what's true. They never have, and they never will. Regardless of this truth, it seems as if everything has been left to be defined by emotions, manipulation, propaganda, or agendas, which has led to cataclysmic confusion and chaos in a myriad of realms.

For starters, we are witnessing psychological chaos all around us. People's mental trajectory has gone astray because truth no longer serves as a baseline for the mind. We also see philosophical chaos as individuals and scholars doodle with ideas and theories ad nauseum. Scripture calls this ever-learning yet never coming to the knowledge of the truth (2 Timothy 3:7). Today people collect information like they used to collect trading cards or limited-edition Beanie Babies.

In order to return to a culture based on God's Word as the ultimate source of truth, we must pursue the knowing of God and His Word with great sincerity and fervor. We must proclaim His Word as much as possible. And we must seek to model His kingdom values in all we say and do.

Reaction: In what ways does consistent time in God's Word help align your thoughts and actions with truth?

How does a removal of God's Word from society impact society's values?

This week, identify and commit to one way that you can increase your awareness and application of God's Word in your own life. Write down what you plan to do.

Prayer: *Jesus, I want to know Your Word more than I do already. Will You give me an increased desire to spend time in Your Word? Show me how practical it is when I apply it to the everyday decisions of my life. I ask that You will open my spiritual eyes so that I can discern truth from lies in what I hear all around me, and do this by primarily rooting more of Your Word in my mind, heart, and soul. In Your name, amen.*

Three

Therefore Pilate entered again into the Praetorium, and summoned Jesus and said to Him, "Are You the King of the Jews?" Jesus answered, "Are you saying this on your own initiative, or did others tell you about Me?" Pilate answered, "I am not a Jew, am I? Your own nation and the chief priests delivered You to me; what have You done?" Jesus answered, "My kingdom is not of this world. If My kingdom were of this world, then My servants would be fighting so that I would not be handed over to the Jews; but as it is, My kingdom is not of this realm." Therefore Pilate said to Him, "So You are a king?" Jesus answered, "You say correctly that I am a king. For this I have been born, and for this I have come into the world, to testify to the truth. Everyone who is of the truth hears My voice." Pilate said to Him, "What is truth?"

John 18:33–38

What our nation needs most right now is a return to Christian character and kingdom values. Without a foundation of truth, character and values carry about as much weight and consistency as the wind that whips across the open plains. Change the definition of *truth* and, by default, you'll have to change the values

13

assigned to it or rising from it. This is because truth is the foundation of character.

But what is truth? Pilate asked the question of our culture when he spoke to Jesus in the passage we are reading today, found in John 18. Pilate asked the same exact question we hear over and over again in arguments and disputes, and especially online: What in the world is truth? And, what's more, who gets to define it?

Social media has become a quagmire of nonsense comprised merely out of the corruption of truth. People post things on social media that couldn't be further from the truth. Yet, because the human mind has been conditioned to believe what it sees in print, there are myriads of people who read it and believe it. It can leave you scratching your head as you scroll from post to post of seemingly contradictory "truth."

Granted, it's hard to know what truth is if you live in a culture that also denies it exists. Many like to claim that truth does not exist, all the while posting "their truth." What that means is that, to them, truth does not exist other than the truth they choose to be true. And if you disagree with "their truth," then you are wrong.

Pilate didn't live in a world of absolutes, either. He was an agnostic. He questioned whether or not anyone could know truth. But rather than point fingers at Pilate, if we were to open our eyes in our Christian culture today, we would find many people exactly like him. That's why it's critical that we become rooted and grounded in the truth of God's Word. This will enable us to sift through the lies of the enemy, as well as to proclaim truth in a world that needs it badly.

Reaction: What methods do you use to sift through what you read on social media, or in the news, in order to find out what is true in it and what is not?

Describe the change in reaction to what used to be considered truth from God's Word and the current cultural response to God's Word overall.

Identify some ways this drifting from God's Word in our culture has led to the breakdown of society.

Prayer: Jesus, I desire and intend to live my life as a kingdom disciple who aligns my thoughts, words, and actions under the umbrella of Your kingdom values. I want to honor You in all that I do, but in order to do that, I need help in sifting through Satan's lies so that I do not become trapped by them. Help me do that so that I can truly live my life as a follower of You, who represents and reflects You fully in what I think, say, and do. In Your name, amen.

15

Four

> So Jesus was saying to those Jews who had believed Him, "If you continue in My word, then you are truly disciples of Mine; and you will know the truth, and the truth will make you free."
>
> John 8:31–32

Truth can be defined as an absolute standard by which reality is measured. Jesus tells us that truth not only exists, but it is also a powerful force when He states in John 8:32, "And you will know the truth, and the truth will make you free." Truth is not a made-up concept. Truth exists. Jesus testifies to its existence and says that you and I can come to know truth for ourselves.

This absolute standard by which reality is measured sits outside of you and me as an objective standard.

As we are looking at this week in our devotions, truth is not based on emotion. I want to revisit this reality because it affects us all more than we realize. Regardless of how you feel about something that is true, you need to keep in mind that your feelings don't determine the truth. Your feelings could be wrong. Truth does not need your emotions to approve it or validate it. One plus one has always equaled two, and it will always equal two. This is because it is a fixed, absolute standard by which reality is to be measured. Without this standard, much of what rests on mathematical formulas and programs would come crashing to a halt. Without this standard, the physics of the universe would collapse, as would the world in which we live.

You must decide, as every Christian should, where you stand on this subject of truth. Now, I didn't say you must decide what is truth. Rather, you must decide where you stand on the subject of truth. You must decide if you are going to fall sway to a culture that allows each person to do what is right in their own eyes, as we see in the book of Judges, or whether you are going to recognize that there is an objective standard by which truth has been established. Contaminated and sinful flesh cannot be relied upon to establish or maintain truth. Sinfulness distorts the truth. Trust rests in the pure perfection of the Creator Himself.

Reaction: Describe a time in your life when you allowed your feelings to dictate what you believed to be true, only to find out after the fact that your feelings were wrong.

What is one key principle you learned from that situation?

What is a good way to check your emotions against the standard of truth revealed in God's Word?

Prayer : Jesus, motivate my heart to lean on Your truth and to know Your truth as the absolute standard that I base my own decisions on. Reward those times in my life when I do that so I can gain insight into how living a life in alignment with You brings about good in my life. Show me what it means to check my emotions against the truth of Your Word and how I can do that as a regular part of my day. In Your name I pray, amen.

Five

In the beginning was the Word, and the Word was with God, and the Word was God. He was in the beginning with God. All things came into being through Him, and apart from Him nothing came into being that has come into being. In Him was life, and the life was the Light of men. The Light shines in the darkness, and the darkness did not comprehend it. . . . And the Word became flesh, and dwelt among us, and we saw His glory, glory as of the only begotten from the Father, full of grace and truth.

John 1:1–5; 14

Jesus came to give us the truth. In Him is the truth. He is truth. This is why Satan and his demons have tried so hard throughout time to get rid of Jesus, or marginalize Him. The light of Christ shines so brightly that darkness has to flee. So instead of taking on a battle they know they will lose, demons seek to deceive people so they never even have a chance to see Christ's light in their lives.

To do this, demons have a school in which most of humanity has enrolled over the years. Scripture calls what they teach there the "doctrines of demons" (1 Timothy 4:1). Satan and his demonic forces seek to trick people with half-truths, partial truths, and all-out lies in order to deceive and control the population. I would imagine that there is not one person reading this book who has not been duped by the devil at one time or another. Satan is the Father of Lies, and he's a master at deception, particularly those cloaked in partial truths. It's far easier to swallow a lie coated in truth than it is without it. The devil knows that is so, which is why you'll often find truth mixed in with lies when he sets out to deceive (Genesis 3:1–6; Matthew 4:1–11).

You and I are living in a worldwide web of lies. Everywhere we look and everywhere we go, we are bombarded with secular, cultural billboards blasting lies. Sure, they may be nicely painted, dressed up, and sophisticated sounding lies, but they are still lies. We live in a land of duplicity that has increasingly drifted away from a Judeo-Christian ethic, ultimately washing ashore onto a liar's paradise. The devil is deceitful, so the culture is contaminated.

If you want to discover absolute truth upon which kingdom values arise, it must come from an absolute source. Perfect truth comes only out of a perfect source. Everything else is guesswork.

And there is only one perfect source in the universe: God.

When you, or anyone you know, disagrees with God, then you are wrong. They are wrong. It is impossible for God to be wrong. God is truth. There are two answers to every question—God's answer and everybody else's. And when everybody else disagrees with God, then everybody else is wrong.

There is nothing in God's nature that even makes it possible for Him to lie. He knows everything about everything. And when you know everything about everything, you can't be wrong. When you know the past, present, and the future, you can't be wrong. When you are the one who made it all to begin with, sustains it all in every moment—you can't be wrong. Jesus declared that as a part of the Triune Godhead, He came "full of grace and truth" (John 1:14).

Reaction: What was something Satan deceived you about that impacted your life in a negative way?

What did you learn through that experience?

How does Jesus' light drive out the darkness of deceit, in practical terms?

Prayer: *Jesus, flood my soul with the light of Your truth so that I will know which way to go in my life in order to live out my kingdom purpose. I do not want to get caught or trapped in Satan's deception. Forgive me for those times when I not only believed the devil's lies but also promoted them through what I did or said. Cover me with Your goodness and grace so that I can walk confidently in the light of Your Word. In Your name I pray, amen.*

Six

> Beloved, do not believe every spirit, but test the spirits to see whether they are from God, because many false prophets have gone out into the world. By this you know the Spirit of God: every spirit that confesses that Jesus Christ has come in the flesh is from God; and every spirit that does not confess Jesus is not from God; this is the spirit of the antichrist, of which you have heard that it is coming, and now it is already in the world.
>
> 1 John 4:1–3

Satan tries to trip us up individually, but he also does so collectively. This is because there are consequences to living a life apart from God's kingdom values. Satan knows that if he can get one person off-track, that person's thoughts, words, and actions will have a negative impact on someone else. So, if Satan can't get to you, he may seek to get to someone you love instead. That's why we need to be prayerful for those we love on a daily basis. We need to pray for protection for them, not just physically but also for spiritual protection.

For example, if one player commits a foul in a football game, the whole team is penalized. That's just how it works. The whole team has to start over. The whole team gets what they just executed wiped from the books. The whole team suffers. We see this play out in Scripture at the start of recorded time when Adam sinned and the whole world fell into chaos. What's true with Adam holds true today, too, in many ways—sin has a way of affecting much more than those in the immediate circle of the sinner. Satan knows the impact of sin and its far-reaching effects. That's why he is so persistent at planting seeds that seek to displace the root of truth in a person's life.

The goal of deception is to keep you away from God. The longer you believe lies, the longer you live apart from God's abiding presence with you, as well as the divine assistance He makes available to you. This is because God cannot partner with or participate in a lie.

Now, lies come in all shapes and sizes. Even the Antichrist will go on to perform great miracles and signs with wonders (2 Thessalonians 2:1–10). A person can be tricked with things that seem good. Have you ever heard the phrase "too good to be true"? Just because something is a miracle doesn't mean it is from God. That's why we are told in 1 John 4:1–3 to "test the spirits" in order to determine and discern which is from God. Just because someone or something sounds good doesn't mean they are good or it is good. Satan is very clever at knowing exactly how to trip you up. He has the playbook on all of us in order to go after us according to our own personal weaknesses.

The chaos in our culture today and the social calamities we face globally are due to the majority of people on this planet watering the seeds of the lies from the devil. For example, our culture believes his lies about homosexuality and gender, family structure, abortion, premarital sex, and many other things. Satan's deception creates confusion as he seeks to redefine what it means to be a man, woman, or family; or what it means to be a certain race or ethnicity; or what it means to be popular, valuable, or significant; or even what it means to be attractive.

Satan subtly erodes the fiber of our futures through redefining the content of what it means to have character. He doesn't want you or me living according to the kingdom values of the kingdom of light. He wants you and me to embrace his kingdom values from his kingdom of darkness. And so he seeks to deceive each of us in our own unique ways, knowing that what may work for one person may not for another.

Reaction: In what way has Satan had a negative impact in your life through the sins of someone else?

Is there something you can do to help remind yourself to pray more consistently for the spiritual protection of your loved ones?

Describe a condition in our culture today that is the result of the consequences of collective sin.

Prayer: *Jesus, I ask that You will cover and protect my loved ones against the schemes of the devil. Open their eyes to see Your truth and to recognize the deceptive strategies of Satan. Bring people into their lives who will speak truth to them. I pray for a hedge of protection against the enemy, not only for myself but for those within my circle of influence. Keep us all from the Evil One, that we may not buy in to his deception. In Your name I pray, amen.*

Seven

But the Spirit explicitly says that in later times some will fall away from the faith, paying attention to deceitful spirits and doctrines of demons, by means of the hypocrisy of liars seared in their own conscience as with a branding iron, men who forbid marriage and advocate abstaining from foods which God has created to be gratefully shared in by those who believe and know the truth.

1 Timothy 4:1–3

Being aware of Satan's opposition to our reflection of God as kingdom disciples is an important part of successfully living out kingdom values. While Satan may come at you like your friend promising you pleasure, notoriety, fame, family, or friends, there is one thing you need to realize from the start: Satan is not on your side. Satan is your enemy. He hates you. He is the opponent. And the reason he hates you so much is because you are made in the image of the One he hates the most: God.

Sure, Satan may sweet-talk you and act like your friend sometimes, but Satan's strategy is always to take you out. Like a football team preparing to face an opponent, Satan has studied you. He has studied your game film. He has dug through the clips to discover what motivates you, triggers you, causes you to act or react in a way that he wants.

In studying you—and in studying each of us—the devil and his demons know which strings to pull or which buttons to push. It's not the same strategy for every believer. No, he's got your specific number and uniquely zeroes in on what it takes to trip you up from living a life marked by kingdom character.

And because Satan and his minions have studied you and know you so well, they will be consistent with bringing to you that which you are most apt to fall into. Sometimes this comes through creating false doctrines, or false rules. Other times it comes through raising up something inside of someone to oppose true doctrine and truth-based virtues.

Whatever the approach, Satan does all he can to get you off-track from fleshing out the kingdom values in your everyday experience. This prevents you from modeling to a lost world what it looks like to reflect the glory of God and His character. One way to overcome Satan's strategies is by being aware of his strategies. Another way is through consistent prayer. As you go to God each day, ask Him to keep you from the Evil One. In doing so, you are asking God to keep you from the wiles of the devil and his attempts to get you off-track.

This concept is modeled for us in the Lord's Prayer and should be a daily routine in our lives.

A third way to overcome Satan's schemes is through living an authentic life before the Lord. Being honest with God about your own sins and shortcomings and being raw with God regarding your own heart will give you a closer relationship with Him. Deceitful spirits and demons prey on those who live inauthentic, hypocritical lives. They prey on those who have had their own conscience seared as with a branding iron through denying their own sins, justifying them, or downplaying them. They prey on those who have lived far enough away from the truth that they no longer even recognize it. And the way they get those who still discern the truth into a position where their conscience no longer works is through subtly steering them away in small increments, like Satan did to Eve when he questioned, "Has God said?"

Reaction: In what ways do you feel that you are successfully overcoming Satan's schemes in your life?

Is there anything you can do to make yourself more aware of Satan's approaches in getting you to live outside of God's character and values? If yes, what would that be?

How does one person reflecting God's glory and values impact society? Can one person really make a difference? If yes, can you give an example?

Prayer : *Jesus, help me live with open eyes and an open heart to the deceptive schemes of Satan. Your kingdom values are rooted in truth, which is why the devil seeks to distort the truth in my own life. Show me how to overcome my own areas of weakness and sin so that I can live a holier, purer, and more committed life to You. I pray this all in Your name, amen.*

Eight

And there was war in heaven, Michael and his angels waging war with the dragon. The dragon and his angels waged war, and they were not strong enough, and there was no longer a place found for them in heaven. And the great dragon was thrown down, the serpent of old who is called the devil and Satan, who deceives the whole world; he was thrown down to the earth, and his angels were thrown down with him. Then I heard a loud voice in heaven, saying,

"Now the salvation, and the power, and the kingdom of our God and the authority of His Christ have come, for the accuser of our brethren has been thrown down, he who accuses them before our God day and night. And they overcame him because of the blood of the Lamb and because of the word of their testimony, and they did not love their life even when faced with death."

Revelation 12:7–11

The only way to identify a lie is to know the truth. But if a person does not know the truth, then the lies will consume him. And before you know it, not only will this person be accepting lies as truth, but this person will also be endorsing them. That's how deep Satan's deception runs. He's clever. He will get a person to die for a lie, all the while condemning and criticizing those who are standing for the truth.

It reminds me of the farmer who had gotten tired of the neighborhood boys coming and stealing his watermelons. After enough times, he decided he would be clever about how he handled it. The farmer decided to put up a sign at the edge of his watermelon garden that read, "One of these watermelons is poisoned." *That'll do it*, the farmer thought, as he wedged his freshly painted sign into the ground.

The problem is that the farmer underestimated the neighborhood boys. When he came out the next day, he saw that the number one had been crossed out with red paint. In its place was painted the number two. While the farmer knew he hadn't poisoned any of the watermelons himself, he didn't know if the boys had, and he wouldn't be able to sell them. The farmer lost his whole crop because he could not outwit the thieves seeking to do him harm.

Satan is a thief who wants nothing more than to do you harm. If you think you are going to somehow outsmart him, outmaneuver him, or outwit him, I would advise you to think again. This isn't his first rodeo, and you aren't his first prey. Satan has been doing this too long. That's why the only way you are going to uncover his lies in your life and reveal his plan to take you down is by taking every thought you have captive to the Word of God. You are to study God's Word and discern what God says on the matter. That should be your first question on every subject: What does God say about it? What God has to say is the absolute truth on the matter.

As you bring up the truth of God's Word in the face of the many issues you may face, Satan will have to retreat. He holds no power or authority over God. In fact, Satan is allergic to Scripture because he's allergic to truth. Like water tossed onto the wicked witch in *The Wizard of Oz*, Satan cannot handle the truth. He dissolves in its presence. As we see in the passage for today from Revelation 12, Satan flees when you call on the blood of Jesus through the power of your testimony rooted in the basic building block of truth in God's Word.

Reaction: On a scale of 1–10, how much of the spiritual "abundant life" do you feel you are experiencing?

1---2---3---4---5---6---7---8---9---10

What things can you do in order to move that number higher on the scale?

Why is spiritual maturity an ongoing pursuit rather than a onetime goal?

Prayer: *Jesus, draw out the plans You have for me from the depths of my understanding into the forefront of my awareness. Help me see the swiftest route to spiritual maturity so that I can take it fully without fail. Give me grace to grow and experience all that I am meant to be, for Your glory and others' good. In Your name, amen.*

Nine

> . . . in that they show the work of the Law written in their hearts, their conscience bearing witness and their thoughts alternately accusing or else defending them . . .
>
> Romans 2:15

We all have equal access to a conscience that helps us know the truth. Our conscience has been given to us to bear witness on what we do and say. It is our conscience that guides us into truth and helps us identify deceptive strategies of Satan.

In fact, your conscience ought to make you feel guilty when you think or do something contrary to the truth. It also ought to make you feel confirmed when you think or do something that aligns with the truth.

If you have ever continued in a practice of sin, you'll know the cycle your conscience goes through. You will start off feeling guilty. But as you continue to move ahead with whatever sinful thought or action you are taking part in, you are suppressing the truth in your own life. You are holding down the manifestation of the truth. You might begin by making excuses. You dismiss any thoughts that say you should stop. Yet eventually your conscience gets so used to what you are doing that you don't need excuses or dismissals anymore. In fact, your conscience becomes so dulled that it no longer even alerts you to the deception you've adopted as truth.

Your conscience started out as a gift from God to serve as a regulator for your human heart. It's a gift that has been given to everyone. That's why even if a person doesn't have a Bible or doesn't attend church— even if they are not a Christian—there are certain behaviors and thoughts that don't make sense or sit well with a conscience. There are certain things that gnaw at a person's internal compass because God has built this truth into all of us. And the only way we remove its influence is through an ongoing suppression of the truth it reflects.

God tells us clearly that we are without an excuse for knowing the Source and Author of truth. God has demonstrated His truth and His presence throughout the majesty of His creation. He has placed in every human heart the knowledge of the reality of His created order. The fact that God knows what He is doing and what He is talking about is evident not only by what He has made, but by what He sustains every moment of every day.

But recognizing there is a God who made everything means we should also recognize there is a God who knows how things should operate within the world He has made. Since God made the world, then He knows how best it should operate and how best we should function within it. If you want to establish your own set of values or rules, then you just need to go make your own world. Yet while you and I live in God's created order, it is best for us to function according to His values and rules. Our conscience is a gift that enables us to know God's rules within us. Paying attention to that internal voice known as your conscience will help you live a life that is pleasing to God and beneficial not only to yourself but also to others.

Reaction: Can you identify a time when your conscience convicted you of sin but you persisted in the thoughts or behavior? What happened to your conscience's conviction of that sin over time?

In what ways does the media or entertainment go about attempting to eliminate the collective conscience toward sin?

Are there areas in your life where you have dulled your conscience that you need to address? If yes, what is one practical step you can take today and this week to address it?

Prayer: *Jesus, forgive me for those areas in my life where I have allowed my conscience to become dull as I continue in sinful thoughts or behaviors. Will You give me wisdom on how I can reactivate my conscience in those areas so that I am sensitive to sin and its effect in my life? I want to please You and honor You with my life choices, so please give me a greater awareness of the areas in my life where I am living contrary to Your kingdom values. In Your name I pray, amen.*

Ten

"For My thoughts are not your thoughts,
Nor are your ways My ways," declares the Lord.
"For as the heavens are higher than the earth,
So are My ways higher than your ways
And My thoughts than your thoughts.
For as the rain and the snow come down from
     heaven,
And do not return there without watering the earth
And making it bear and sprout,
And furnishing seed to the sower and bread to the
     eater;
So will My word be which goes forth from My
     mouth;
It will not return to Me empty,
Without accomplishing what I desire,
And without succeeding in the matter for which I
     sent it."

Isaiah 55:8–11

Far too many people treat the Bible like they do the monarchy of England. They'll give the institution some props. They'll post about it on social media. They'll let others know that they appreciate it. But they will not give it any power because it does not have the final say-so. It does not affect their decisions, emotions, and direction. Similarly, until you and I, and our culture as a whole, develop a radical understanding of Scripture's authority in our lives, it will be of little use to us.

Scripture is the revelation of God. It is God's primary way of disclosing to us all that He wants us to know and how we are to live. Seeing truth in Scripture can be compared to sitting in a theater and having someone pull back the curtain so you can see what's behind it. Scripture reveals to us the whole story. It is God giving you and me the content He wants us to have in order to guide us, lead us, and show us the best ways forward. As He says in Isaiah 55, His Word has a purpose. His Word will accomplish what He desires, and that is because His Word has the authoritative power of truth.

The reason we need to pay attention to Him and His Word more than we pay attention to anything else is because God reveals His heart and His thoughts to us in it. And we can't guess what God is thinking or assume we know what He is thinking because He doesn't think like us. His thoughts are not our thoughts. He doesn't roll like us. His ways are not our ways. In fact, God's ways are not even close to our ways. As high as the heaven stretches above the earth is how different we are from God. We are finite. We think of things from a finite, limited perspective. God is infinite. He knows all.

Anytime you or I try to figure something out independently of God, we start down the pathway of confusion. God operates and functions on a whole other level. When we align our thoughts with Him, we discover the peaceful gift of clarity. This is because the words that proceed out of God's mouth are not just empty speech. He speaks purposefully. God is always intentional.

It's like if you were stuck in a maze or an escape room and you called to one of the employees for help. When you called for help, they would give you a clue. They would give you guidance. They would give you information that you would not have known on your own. The reason they can give it is because they know the way out. They know the path you need to take to reach your destination. God has disclosed in Scripture all you need to know to reach your divine destiny. He has revealed the truth you need to live out a life that is reflective of His character and kingdom values. When you live this way, you will fulfill the purpose He has for you, and you will impact our culture and our nation for good.

Reaction: What happens when you fail to study God's Word and meditate on it?

Have you ever assumed to know what God was thinking, only to discover His plan went beyond your scope of thought? If yes, describe what principle you learned in that process.

How can you apply the principle you learned from the second reaction question into a situation you are struggling with today?

Prayer: Father, Your thoughts go beyond me at such a high level that I shouldn't even try to presume that I know Your plans. Help me walk by faith as I trust in the revelation You give me each step of the way. Guide me into Your plan and purpose for my life as I draw closer to You in a heart of worship and trust. I pray all of this in Jesus' name, amen.

Eleven

> I testify to everyone who hears the words of the prophecy of this book: if anyone adds to them, God will add to him the plagues which are written in this book.
>
> Revelation 22:18

God's Word is pure, undefiled truth. Yet you and I live in a post-truth world. We live in a world that prefers deception facilitated by evil. In fact, many Christians prefer deception facilitated by evil because it makes them feel good. Adding anything to God's Word is never a good idea. Merging God's truth with some other idea leads only to falsities. God's Word is what will stand the test of time, trends, and trials.

Jesus declared that even heaven and earth would pass away before the smallest detail in the Word of God would not be fulfilled. We read Jesus' words in Matthew 5:18, "For truly I say to you, until heaven and earth pass away, not the smallest letter or stroke shall pass from the Law until all is accomplished." The "letter or stroke" Jesus refers to are the smallest markings in the Hebrew alphabet. He tells us that the Scripture is so complete, comprehensive, and true that the tiniest strokes of it will be fulfilled—every last detail.

In fact, God warns us in Revelation 22:18 that anyone who adds to Scripture, or takes away from it, will be bringing plagues upon themselves. It is God who is protecting, covering, and preserving His Word.

But until we discover our need to turn to the truth of God's Word over the lies of the world, we will never solve the cultural, racial, relational, political, or myriad other problems plaguing our nation today. Until we discover what it means to truly abide in and align under the truth of God's Word, we will continue to experience the chaos and confusion that currently engulfs us.

Jesus told us clearly in John 8:31 that those who abide in the truth of His words are truly His disciples. If you flip that, it makes it clear that when you do not abide in Christ's Word and align under the truth, you are not a kingdom disciple. To *abide* means to hang out, loiter, or remain in. For example, you abide in your home. You live there. To abide in the truth of Christ, you need to live with His perspective. You need to live according to His worldview. It means to live with a desire to know what Jesus feels, thinks, and says on the subject you are dealing with.

You cannot be His disciple and ignore His Word. You cannot be His disciple and reject His Word. You can't say you are a kingdom disciple yet not hold God's inherent Word in high esteem. The two are mutually exclusive.

What's missing in our culture today are Christians who will stand on His Word with the right attitude and right spirit of kindness and humility, but also with crystal-clear clarity as to what it says because His Word is flawless. His Word makes no mistakes on anything it talks about or addresses, and it addresses everything we need to know. Yet in our post-Christian environment, respect for God's Word may be the most you get. Not yielding to it. Not aligning under it. Not being governed by it. And this is why we are living in the chaos that consumes us today.

Reaction: Describe what it means to you in contemporary and practical terms to abide in God's Word.

How do you think abiding in God's Word positively impacts your own life?

In what ways do you think drawing even closer to God's Word could bring improvements into your life?

Prayer: Jesus, forgive me for having pulled back from Your Word and failing to abide in it as I should. I know that Your Word contains truth, and yet I seem to scroll through the deceptions of the world far more frequently than spending time in Your Word. Open my eyes and heart to my own *shortcomings when it comes to truly abiding in Your truth. Your Word is a light to my path. Help me not to stumble in darkness any longer, but to walk according to the truth laid out for me in Your Word. In Your name I pray, amen.*

Twelve

Your word is a lamp to my feet
And a light to my path.

Psalm 119:105

One day a man went to visit a doctor because he wasn't feeling well. The doctor performed his examination and then prescribed some medication for the man to take. The doctor even had the nurse call in the prescription to the local pharmacy, where the man went and picked it up. A week later, the man called the doctor and complained that he was still sick. The doctor asked how much of the medication he had taken. "I haven't taken any," the man replied. "I haven't opened it."

The doctor responded, "Well, that's your problem. Take it. And don't call me again until you do."

A lot of us will pick up the Bible and carry it under our arm. Or we'll pick up a Bible and put it on the side table or by our bed. We'll pick up our Bible and yet fail to open it to see what is inside. We won't open it to read, discern, learn, and be impacted by its truth. Yet when we fail to treat Scripture as the absolute, inerrant, authoritative voice of God in print, it is we who will pay the price. We will pay the price in our lives, relationships, work, finances, peace of mind, and so

47

much more. The things that plague us will only increase when we neglect to learn and apply God's truth to the situations and challenges we face.

One day I was in my car and the side mirror collapsed. I couldn't get it to open back up to where it was supposed to be. So I decided to figure it out. I fiddled with that mirror, pushed that mirror, pulled that mirror, sought to maneuver that mirror for close to twenty minutes. I knew I couldn't drive without a mirror to show me the cars behind and beside me, so I stayed with the situation, seeking a solution.

Eventually, it dawned on me that in the glove box of my car was a book, the car's manual. Now, honestly speaking, I hadn't opened that book before, even though I owned it. I hadn't read that book, even though it was close by me all the time I drove. I had become so satisfied with the basics that I never explored the book.

Until I was stuck. Until I couldn't go anywhere. Until I needed that book. So, this time, I grabbed the book. It didn't take me too long to figure out how to fix my mirror once I decided to use the book that was designed exactly for that purpose—to help me drive my car.

It wasn't until stuff wasn't working for me and my human understanding couldn't figure it out anymore that I remembered the manufacturer of my car had made a book for me to use. In hindsight, I wasted a lot of time and experienced a lot of frustration just because I put off going to the one place that held the answer to my problem.

Likewise, many believers today are wasting a lot of time and experiencing a lot of frustration because they refuse to go to the one place that holds the answers to any problems they face. If they, or we as the body of Christ, would simply return to the Source of truth as our source of truth and then do what it says, we could solve the issues creating the chaos around us and within us.

Reaction: What does it mean to you personally to "return to the Source of truth as our source of truth"?

What is the foundational principle to "returning to the Source of truth as our source of truth"? In other words, what must take place in order for this to happen?

In what areas would you like to see God give you greater grace or favor in your life?

Prayer: *Jesus, reveal to me the ways to please You so that I can experience a greater level of Your favor and grace in my life. Help me to always stay close to Your Word so that I can stand on the foundation of knowing what truth is. I don't want to be deceived by culture, friends, or family members, so give me a greater level of discernment to spot the lies and inconsistencies in what I'm hearing all around me. In Your name I pray, amen.*

Thirteen

And we also thank God continually because, when you received the word of God, which you heard from us, you accepted it not as a human word, but as it actually is, the word of God, which is indeed at work in you who believe.

1 Thessalonians 2:13 NIV

In order for the word of truth to work in building kingdom virtue in our lives, it must be received. It must be believed. We must allow humility to enter our hearts in such a way that we understand God is the Author of truth, and we are not.

For God's Word to have its way in us and do what it was designed and revealed to accomplish, you must welcome it in. If and when you don't do that, it doesn't change the truth from being the truth. It just changes the power of the truth in how it works for you.

When we talk about receiving it, keep in mind that it's the truth of God that you need to receive. It doesn't necessarily mean what a preacher said, or even a biblical scholar, or what was printed in a Christian magazine. Many people peddle the Word out of a wrong motivation or are simply misguided themselves while their motives may be pure.

Paul urged Timothy to stick with the truth in 2 Timothy 4:1–5 (NIV). Just like in our day, there were people in Paul's day seeking to say what "itching ears" wanted to hear. Good-sounding, popular myths fill pulpits all across our nation because so many people have abandoned the truth. Far too many people simply want to be placated. They want to be made to feel good. They want a doughnut sermon. A doughnut sermon is that which satisfies the taste buds. It tickles the taste but has no nutritional value.

Too many people want doughnut Christianity—a religion that makes them feel good, while being void of truth. But they don't mind if it is void of truth because they just like how it sounds and how it feels.

But you and I, as kingdom disciples, are to be people of the truth. In order to be people of the truth, we must be people of the Word. We must be people of Scripture. We must make God's Word our guide for our thoughts, words, and actions. When we do that, we will discover the powerful, transformative impact His Word will apply to our lives, our surroundings, and our nation.

An airplane needs a control tower in order to direct the pilot to the final destination, as well as to keep the pilot and passengers from harm's way. Similarly, a life on earth needs a control tower. There are many times this world gets cloudy, stormy, overrun, and dangerous.

There are many times when you cannot see the place where you are headed or the disastrous paths around you. But if you will look to God's Word for teaching, correction, and direction, you will know how to navigate the challenges and chaos of this world. The Bible is our control tower. It is our source of all truth.

When you and I learn that we must treat God's Word as it was created to be treated—not just something to make you feel good when you pick or choose a passage to read—is when it will become profitable in our lives and in our land.

Reaction: When you read the Bible, do you tend to go to those passages that support what you are already thinking? How do you respond to the passages that convict you or disagree with your way of thinking?

Is there an idea or thought-construct within you that God's Word continually seeks to convict and correct? If so, what is it, and are you open to yielding it to the truth?

Take some time to ask God to intervene in your heart and mind and reveal areas where you need the light of His Word to guide you.

Prayer : *Father, I believe Your Word is true, but sometimes I avoid it. Or at least, I avoid those places in it that convict me of wrong thoughts or wrong actions. Forgive me for distancing Your Word from my life so that I don't have to do the uncomfortable work of changing my life to align all of it under You. Thank You for the grace of Your forgiveness. In Jesus' name, amen.*

Fourteen

> Peter said to Him, "Explain the parable to us." Jesus said, "Are you still lacking in understanding also? Do you not understand that everything that goes into the mouth passes into the stomach, and is eliminated? But the things that proceed out of the mouth come from the heart, and those defile the man. For out of the heart come evil thoughts, murders, adulteries, fornications, thefts, false witness, slanders. These are the things which defile the man; but to eat with unwashed hands does not defile the man."
>
> Matthew 15:15–20

There are many ways to gauge your own personal kingdom virtue, but the primary one is in what you say. Your mouth reveals your heart.

When you go to the doctor, they will often ask you to stick out your tongue. They do this because they are looking for things on your tongue that could indicate something wrong deeper inside you. The Bible declares that a person's speech also reveals whether or not there is something wrong deeper inside him or her. What you say, and how you say it, reflects your heart within. James 1:26 puts it like this: "If anyone thinks himself to be religious, and yet does not bridle his tongue but deceives his own heart, this man's religion is worthless."

Basically, if you can't control your tongue, your "religion is worthless." Now, I understand that occasionally you and I will make mistakes. But what Paul is referring to is the ongoing process and revelation of spiritual maturity. If your normal mode of operation is to belittle, judge, gossip, scorn, mock, lie, or use any other verbal vice known to mankind, then you may want to reconsider where your relationship sits with Jesus Christ.

The things that are spoken by you, or by anyone for that matter, come from the heart. What you say, and how you say it, reveals the real you. The kingdom of God ought to reflect God's kingdom virtues. But instead it seems a shift has occurred. We are being inundated with information and communication modeled after Facebook posts, Instagram feeds, Twitter rants, chats, messaging, memes, and more. We've got unhealthy communication going every which way. Not only is it often full of lies, but it is also just as frequently full of angst and evil ways of communicating with or about others.

As kingdom followers, we are to be speaking the truth in love. We are to speak according to the absolute standard by which reality is measured. Or, to put it another way, we are to speak that which reflects

God's view on any subject. It doesn't matter how many people agree with you. It doesn't matter how many people like what you have to say. It doesn't even matter how you might feel about it. Once God says something is true, it is to dominate the environment and atmosphere of His people because we are seeking to function according to His kingdom worldview.

You may want to examine where you are today as opposed to where you were several months or a year ago. Has your mouth (what you say, how you say it, and why you choose to say it) fallen more in line with going between the two goalposts of truth and love, or are you still speaking from the flesh? This is how you can know if you are growing in godly character and kingdom virtues.

Reaction: Do you want to "have the last word," or are you willing to let things slide for the sake of love and kindness?

Do you speak as if what you say is the end-all-be-all on every topic, or do you leave room open to someone possibly knowing more than you do?

Do your words reflect a heart of fear or faith, calm or chaos, peace or pride?

Prayer : *Jesus, help me glorify You with what I say. I want my words to reflect a heart of faith, calm, and peace, so please begin by working in my heart to cultivate these kingdom virtues. I know that what I say reveals my heart, so purify my heart with Your love and kindness. I love You, Jesus, and want my mouth to mature to a level that pleases You. In Your name I ask this, amen.*

Fifteen

As a result, we are no longer to be children, tossed here and there by waves and carried about by every wind of doctrine, by the trickery of men, by craftiness in deceitful scheming; but speaking the truth in love, we are to grow up in all aspects into Him who is the head, even Christ, from whom the whole body, being fitted and held together by what every joint supplies, according to the proper working of each individual part, causes the growth of the body for the building up of itself in love.

Ephesians 4:14–16

Have you ever been to the zoo and seen a wild animal behind bars in a cage? The reason they have the wild animal behind bars is because it is dangerous. Similarly, the tongue is dangerous. That is why the tongue comes caged in what we call a mouth, behind some bars we call our teeth. Yes, the tongue can be a tool for transformation and impact, but far too often it is used as a tool to tear down. We are to speak truth, but we are to speak it with a heart of love. Truth must always be balanced with love.

One of God's greatest attributes is love. It's part of His innate being. God is love. Yet so many of us don't fully grasp what love means. It's a word that is often thrown around in a nonchalant way. So, let me define *love* biblically. Love is the decision to compassionately, righteously, and responsibly seek the well-being of another. It is a decision, not only a feeling. The reason I say it is a decision is because it is commanded by God. A command demands obedience. Love always starts off with a decision. It is a decision to compassionately, righteously, and responsibly do or say something for the betterment of someone else.

This means we are to speak the truth in such a way that the person we are speaking to knows our intention is to seek out what is best for them. We are telling them what we are telling because we want what will be good for them. Obviously, venting would not fall in that category. Neither would gossip, insults, or insinuations. When you and I communicate, according to God's standards on speech, we must communicate in such a way that seeks to help. We must communicate in such a way so as to make something, or someone, better. People should know how much we care for their well-being when we communicate with them.

Now, that doesn't mean to dumb down the truth, but neither does it mean we are to eradicate any concern. When you come across believers you know who are believing or living or saying something errant—who are sinning—they need to know the truth, yes.

But they also need to know the reason you are telling them is because you care for them. You are seeking to keep them from the consequences of an errant way. You are not judging just to judge. You are directing them toward God's perspective on the matter in a manner seasoned with grace.

Love does not tolerate all views. Love is not acquiescing to lies. Christians are to love all people, but we are not called to love all ideas. God makes a clear difference between the sin and the sinner. God loves the sinner. He does not love the sin. Neither does He conflate the two to be the same thing. For example, a loving parent does not accept their child's wrong behavior, and yet they still love their child. And if they are a good parent, they treat their child with love even if they have to correct them. We are always to make a distinction between the action and the person.

We are to love the immoral person. We are not to love immorality. We are to love racists. We are not to love racism. We are to love the angry person. We are not to love anger. The problem today is that the world has attempted to shut down biblical influence in our culture by conflating the two. They are saying that to reject a sin is to make you intolerant. But we are never to be intolerant toward another person made in the image of God. Yet we are also never to deny the truth out of a desire for acceptance. We are to speak the truth in love so that people know we care about their well-being.

Reaction: Why is it important to speak the truth in love?

Describe the two different responses someone may have to hearing hard truths spoken in love versus hard truths spoken in judgment or condemnation.

What would help you better be able to express truth in love when you are talking?

Prayer: *Jesus, create in me a heart of love so that whatever I say to anyone, it is coming from a space of love in me. I want my words to matter to others, so I want them to be seasoned with grace, peace, and love. Remind me in those times I feel passionate about a subject that what I say will best be heard if it is done in a spirit of love. In Your name I pray, amen.*

Sixteen

> Little children, let us not love with word or with tongue, but in deed and truth. We will know by this that we are of the truth, and will assure our heart before Him in whatever our heart condemns us; for God is greater than our heart and knows all things. Beloved, if our heart does not condemn us, we have confidence before God; and whatever we ask we receive from Him, because we keep His commandments and do the things that are pleasing in His sight.
>
> 1 John 3:18–22

One of the best ways to get your prayers answered is to merge truth with love. That means you cannot be a silo saint. You can't be a stay-at-home follower of Jesus Christ. And I'm not talking about just coming to church or going to a sanctuary, either. You need to be engaged with others on a regular basis so that you first have the opportunity to speak the truth in love. When you are touching people and encouraging them to build kingdom virtue in their lives, God sees that you are doing that which is "pleasing in His sight."

So many people feel free today to correct, judge, teach, or blame people they may not even know on social media. But truth spoken in a spirit and context of love is most often in an environment of relationships. In order to have relationships, you need to intentionally set out to connect with others. You need to know people well enough to know when the truth might be needed in their lives. You can't do that if you are never around anybody. The church has many purposes, but one of them is to provide a context for fellowship among believers to take place.

Far too many people wound up using COVID as an excuse to not attend church once the lockdown measures had lifted. They found it far too convenient to watch a sermon on YouTube and call it a day. But church was never meant to simply be a sermon-dispenser, like a Redbox where you get DVDs. Church is a place to connect with others in such a way that everyone can experience God together as we serve Him and get to know Him, and each other, better.

What's more, when you are involved in the lives of people—and you allow people to be involved in your life as well—you are given opportunities to speak the truth in love. You don't have to demand to have your voice heard. You don't have to shout. You don't have to use all caps.

God has given us a community in which we can all thrive when we come together on the basis of two foundational virtues of truth and love. Merging the sharing of truth with love opens the doorway to a greater experience of God in your life. And couldn't we all use a bit more of experiencing the greatness of God in our lives? God's presence casts out fear. His presence calms the chaos. God's presence ushers in peace, hope, and joy. God allows you and me to feel more of His love from Him when He sees that we are willing to share His love, and His truth, with others.

But what's more is that when you and I make it our lifestyle to live with kingdom virtues on the foundation of truth merged with a spirit of love, more of our prayers get answered, too. As we reflect God more in what we say and how we say it—God is more attuned to our prayers.

Reaction: What are some prayer requests you have given to God that have not been addressed yet?

Are any of these prayers possibly being hindered through a lack of love in your own heart combined with a lack of aligning with God's truth?

In what ways can you speak the truth in love to a greater degree?

Prayer: *Jesus, it isn't always easy to merge truth with love. It's far easier to judge, blame, or criticize at times. But I want to honor You with my lifestyle and live according to Your kingdom values. Help me do the difficult work of purifying my own heart and motives while leaning more deeply into love, empathy, and kindness. Soften my heart to feel a greater level of compassion toward those around me. In Your name I pray, amen.*

Seventeen

Now when Jesus saw the crowds, he went up on a mountainside and sat down. His disciples came to him, and he began to teach them.

Matthew 5:1–2 NIV

Living a lifestyle of kingdom values ushers in blessings and favor. When Jesus spoke in what is now called the Sermon on the Mount, He did so because He wanted each of us to know the upside of kingdom values. He also wanted to emphasize that choosing to embrace kingdom values isn't just something you do so you can check off a list. It isn't just something you do so you can post virtue-signaling statements online. Neither is it about "grinning and bearing it" as you seek to live the Christian life. Rather, Jesus paired up each of the kingdom values with a blessing that is to boomerang right back to you.

Instead of living a life of chaos, you'll discover calm. Instead of wandering aimlessly in pain, you will find comfort. Instead of going through life unsatisfied, you will find what you need when you need it most. In these eight different statements on kingdom values that Jesus mentioned in His Sermon on the Mount, Jesus also provided the purpose behind living them out.

I imagine Jesus gave us the purpose because He knows we are human. He knows we need a tangible motivation to spur us on. So He gives us an incentive. He reminds us that when we choose to live and be shaped according to kingdom values, we will be accessing the blessings of God's kingdom for ourselves.

The kingdom values Jesus spoke on in His Sermon on the Mount outline both the responsibility and benefits of living in the kingdom. In fact, in the first twelve verses of His famous sermon, Jesus used the word *blessing*, or a form of it, nine times. On nine separate occasions, we discover what we need to do (what kingdom values we need to live by) in order to receive kingdom blessings. These nine references to blessings cover eight specific values that God desires for us to live by.

You may wonder what this sermon preached so long ago has to do with any of us right now. But the principles in His sermon still apply today. They are principles that, if followed, will shape us into who we need to be as kingdom followers of Christ. When Jesus spoke to His disciples on the mountain that day, He chose His words in such a way so as to elevate them personally to a higher level of kingdom discipleship. But what was relevant to them was also relevant to the additional people gathered nearby, and it remains relevant to all of us right now.

A life of kingdom living that produces kingdom blessing allows you to experience the benefits of the kingdom internally. Without a doubt, that is a relevant pursuit for all of us right now. We could all use a bit more blessing in our lives. That's why Jesus urged us to live as His kingdom disciples, modeling a life of kingdom values in all we say and do.

Reaction: Describe the difference between a blessing from God and a human reward.

In what ways can focusing on human rewards and accolades actually remove the experience of blessings in your life?

What do you think is the main reason it is easier to focus on human rewards and accolades rather than to pursue God's blessings?

Prayer: *Jesus, help mold my mind to distinguish between human rewards and divine blessings so that I will know which I am to pursue. Help me apply the principles You taught in the Sermon on the Mount to such a degree in my life that they become natural to me. I want to walk in the goodness and favor of God's blessings, so enable me to align my heart, mind, and actions under You as the Lord of my life. In Your name I pray, amen.*

Eighteen

"Everyone who hears these words of Mine and does not act on them, will be like a foolish man who built his house on the sand. The rain fell, and the floods came, and the winds blew and slammed against that house; and it fell—and great was its fall."

Matthew 7:26–27

Many people have different ideas about what it means to be blessed. Let's define the term *blessing* from a biblical standpoint. A blessing is a state of well-being where kingdom followers of Christ both enjoy and extend the goodness of God in their lives. A state of well-being refers to your normative way of being. It's not a moment of happiness here, nor is it a burst of energy or enthusiasm there. It refers to your ongoing modus operandi. It's a way of life, not an event.

This state of well-being and divine favor and spiritual stability, also known as *joy* in Scripture, is referred to in the Bible as an inner river that keeps flowing even in times of drought. The work of the Holy Spirit is to produce this in a believer's life. Part of our role in cooperating with our own growth and maturity is to choose to live by the kingdom values outlined for us in the Word of God.

A joyless Christian, if that is his or her normal state of being, indicates that he or she is not very close with the Holy Spirit. Because when you or I abide in Christ, and thus abide in His Spirit, it is the role of the Spirit to fill us with this inner river—this water overflowing with joy.

The Greek word used for *blessed* in the Sermon on the Mount is the word *makarios*. This name referred to Makairos Island, which was off the coast of Greece. It was known at that time as the "blessed island." The reason why they called it blessed was because it was self-contained. The residents who lived there didn't need to leave the island in order to get their needs met because the island offered everything they could ever need to use. The natural resources of this blessed island were so rich, fruitful, productive, and thick that those who lived there had all they needed in order to enjoy their lives to the fullest. They were self-sustained and self-contained without having to go and search for anything else.

In the biblical concept of being blessed, you will discover all you need to live a fulfilled and satisfied life. In the biblical world of being blessed, you ought to be okay to live on an island. Just being with the King surrounded by His kingdom ought to stir up within you an awareness of how blessed you really are. But far too many believers today feel the urge to go somewhere, buy something, change homes, change jobs, change mates, change cars, change churches in a constant search for something outside them to satisfy them, rather than remaining content on the island of God's kingdom blessings.

One of the ways you know that you aren't blessed in the biblical sense of the term is that you have to keep leaving the island to have any amount of satisfaction. You have to leave the island to find peace. You have to leave the island to have happiness. You have to leave the island to feel significance. Anyone who does not recognize what they have with Christ and His kingdom blessings will have to leave the island in a constant search for more.

If you find yourself running all around town trying to find or experience your blessing, you are looking in the wrong location. As a kingdom follower of Jesus Christ, you already have access to your blessing within. You are already on the island called "blessed." You just need to open your spiritual eyes and discover what God has for you.

Reaction: Describe the cause-and-effect relationship between obedience and spiritual blessing.

Why do you think God provided an incentive for obedience?

On a scale of 1–10 (with 10 being the most), where would you rate your life with regard to receiving spiritual blessings? What could you do to move that number closer to 10?

1---2---3---4---5---6---7---8---9---10

Prayer : *Jesus, I want to live with an open flow from heaven of Your blessings and favor. I want to know what it means to live in a state of peace and joy. Show me how to honor You more with an obedient lifestyle and give me greater opportunities for serving You. Show me areas in my life that I need to work on to better align them to Your Word and Your will. In Your name I pray, amen.*

Nineteen

And Jesus came up and spoke to them, saying, "All authority has been given to Me in heaven and on earth."

Matthew 28:18

Living according to kingdom values leads to a life filled with kingdom blessings. It's as simple, and as difficult, as that. I say that it is simple because it is pretty straightforward. There aren't any hoops to jump through. But it is also difficult because we make it difficult through our rebellion, stubbornness, and desire to "find our own way."

Jesus is *the* way to living a blessed life. He knows the way we should go in order to experience the blessings of His kingdom. Just as He spoke to His disciples on the mountainside overlooking the expansive Sea of Galilee, He speaks to us today through His message.

Not too long ago I was able to visit Israel with my family and ministry partners of The Urban Alternative. One of the highlights of the trip was going up on the mountain where Jesus sat down to teach His disciples and the mass of people gathered to hear. As I stood on the mountainside alongside the film crew and my family, I took a moment to look out over the terrain and imagine what it might have looked like with everyone gathered together. I could picture Jesus sitting down on a large stone in order to teach, and the crowd growing quiet. In Matthew 5:1, we read that Jesus sat down to teach. He sat down when He taught on the hillside.

It could have been that Jesus sat down because He was tired. Or it might have been because He knew He was about to speak for a relatively long time. Or it could also have been symbolic. To sit and teach in those days, as it is in our day to a large extent, was to do so from a seat of authority. Like a king sitting on his throne to rule over his kingdom, or the pope speaking *ex cathedra*—meaning "from the chair"—or a judge sitting over a case, it means to speak from authority.

So, when Jesus spoke of kingdom values, know that He did so from a position of authority. No one has more authority than He does to deliver the kingdom principles by which we are to live. He is the King of kings. He owns and rules the world we call our home. And since He does, He knows how we are to live in it as kingdom disciples.

It's important to rest in the knowledge of His authority because that awareness can give you confidence. It can strengthen your resolve to fully follow Jesus Christ. When you know that someone is in authority, you typically take them more seriously. The reason is because authority comes with the ability to hand out blessings or consequences. Thus, when we recognize that Jesus sits in authority over all created beings, it gives us greater motivation to obey Him.

Spending time in Israel in the proximity of where Jesus walked made a huge impact on my life. It helped me recognize the closeness Jesus must have had with His disciples as He walked the roads with them. Sitting down to teach them wasn't so much a prepared and staged event as it was Jesus sharing from His heart in such a way so as to improve the lives of His listeners. He wanted to improve their lives because He loved them. Similarly, Jesus wants to improve our lives today because He loves us. It is only when we begin to understand Jesus' heart of love for us that we find His commandments and guidance freeing in our lives rather than constricting. Living with kingdom values is the surest way to living a life of joy, peace, and abundance—which is exactly what Jesus longs for you to experience (John 10:10).

Reaction: How does Jesus' love for you show up in your life?

Do you find you respond more favorably and intentionally or less favorably when interfacing with someone in authority unbacked by love? Explain why you answered the way you did.

How can you shift from robotic obedience, such as checking off a list, to obeying Jesus out of love in your heart for Him?

Prayer : Jesus, I want to know and experience Your love for me like You shared with Your disciples. I want to know what it is like to walk intimately with You as a friend. As I get to know You more, my heart will respond to You and Your authority because I will also feel Your love. I can trust Your authority when I know You truly love me. Help me come to know Your love on a deeper level than ever before. In Your name I pray, amen.

Twenty

"Blessed are the poor in spirit, for theirs is the kingdom of heaven."

Matthew 5:3

The first kingdom value Jesus chose to focus on in His powerful Sermon on the Mount shows up in verse 3. We read, "Blessed are the poor in spirit, for theirs is the kingdom of heaven" (Matthew 5:3). It's a short statement, but it contains a world of truth. Jesus begins by telling us we are blessed when we are poor. Now, I know that nobody in their right mind likes being poor. If you are a person who loves being poor, you've probably got a problem. Sure, some people can't help but be poor, but it's usually not because they want to be poor.

Many of us grew up poor. I did. I'm sure many of you reading this book did, as well. We grew up without much at all. Some of us grew up eating mayonnaise sandwiches. A mayonnaise sandwich is just that—some bread with some mayo on it. That's all. And if your mom was finally able to get some meat to go on the sandwich, it was the bologna that would bubble up in the middle. Some of us also grew up with government-issued cheese or beans, or government-issued powdered milk.

I'm sure some of you reading this book know exactly what I'm talking about. I'm also sure if you know what I'm talking about, you didn't exactly want to be in the condition you were in at that time. You wanted something better. You wanted a different level of freedom, a greater level of means to progress in life. You wanted something more comfortable than being enmeshed in poverty. And no one would blame you for wanting that.

But that's not the poverty Jesus spoke about. Jesus spoke of a spiritual poverty. What's more, He spoke of it in a way that declared this spiritual poverty to be absolutely essential.

He started His revolutionary sermon by saying something revolutionary to everyone listening at that time, and still today: "Blessed are the poor in spirit . . ." That last part of the phrase is key. Jesus was pronouncing a blessing on spiritual poverty. Spiritual poverty is about humility before God. It's understanding where you are in relationship to Him—that He is the God of the universe, and you belong to Him. He wasn't condemning money. He wasn't condemning the acquisition of land, animals, or even stuff for a home.

In fact, many of God's choicest servants in Scripture were wealthy by today's standards. Many of them would be considered multimillionaires today. Abraham would have fit into that category. David would have fit into that category. Job was definitely in that category. And there was even at least one billionaire in there, too: Solomon. God had no problem with giving His people financial prosperity in the Bible.

But what He did have a problem with, as indicated by Jesus' opening statement, is using your stuff—or your wealth—to measure your spiritual status. For someone to think that God must be closer to them or love them more than the next person just because they have a nice car is to be deceived and void of the true values of the kingdom. Believing that God favors them more than others and is on their side just because they have a better job than the average Joe is to have missed the meaning of life itself. A person can be very success-ful in the physical realm and yet be one of God's worst enemies. Material success does not equate to spiritual success. Sometimes the two can coincide simultane-ously, but that is not always the case and should never be assumed.

Jesus reminded His disciples and those listening that to be blessed in God's kingdom means to intentionally embrace a life that is poor in spirit.

Reaction: Describe the difference between material success and spiritual success.

What are some things Satan uses to try to trick us into believing that material success is the same as spiritual success, if not even better?

How can you overcome Satan's strategies to keep you from embracing a heart that is poor in spirit?

Prayer: *Jesus, I want to embrace a heart and attitude that is poor in spirit. I do not want to live with puffed-up pride and so offend You and Your holiness. Reveal to me the areas in my life where pride has kept me from this right heart and humility. Help me understand the nature of what it means to be truly poor in spirit as I seek to align my life under You. In Your name I pray, amen.*

Twenty-One

For thus says the high and exalted One
Who lives forever, whose name is Holy,
"I dwell on a high and holy place,
And also with the contrite and lowly of spirit
In order to revive the spirit of the lowly
And to revive the heart of the contrite."

Isaiah 57:15

To be poor in spirit is to declare spiritual bankruptcy. We all know that a person declares bankruptcy when they are unable to pay for what they have. When they are no longer able to meet their obligations, they will file bankruptcy. Similarly, living according to the kingdom value of being poor in spirit comes through recognizing our total insufficiency to satisfy what is needed in our own humanity to prosper spiritually.

The problem is that most of us do not recognize our own spiritual insufficiency.

Now, it's easy to recognize if you can't pay your bills. But most of us have a hard time realizing we don't have what it takes to make ends meet spiritually. We can't cover what is needed spiritually for us to mature, be impactful, access blessings, and prosper in our souls. Unfortunately, most of us believe we are far more capable than we actually are. All that does is keep us on the hamster wheel, spinning and spinning in our spiritual cycles. We stay in cycles of reading our Bibles, attending church, or crossing off our prayer lists, only to discover we aren't making any progress at all. But Jesus didn't start out His sermon by saying, "Blessed are those who cross off their spiritual lists." No, He started by saying, "Blessed are the poor in spirit, for theirs is the kingdom of heaven" (Matthew 5:3).

What Jesus says is if we will recognize that our spiritual strength, sufficiency, and abilities are rooted and grounded in Him—because we are poor in spirit—then we will be able to overcome the myriad of things that seem to be coming at us.

Whether it's depression coming at you, or a feeling of defeat, isolation, or grief, or just an overall sense of aimlessness—whatever it is cannot be overcome by you. It is overcome through Christ in you when you recognize His all-sufficiency as King and Lord of all. The world may tell you there's no hope. It may tell you that you will be depressed or a failure for the rest of your life. It may tell you there is no future for you. But what you must remember, if you are poor in spirit, is that the world doesn't have the last word. God does. And whatever Satan is using to seek to overcome you, God can overcome when you look to Him to do it.

Knowing this is true, you should always remember that when God puts you in a situation you cannot fix—no matter how much money you have, or intelligence you have, or power you possess—He is doing you a favor. He is showing you your insufficiency so that you can see the kingdom of heaven at work on your behalf.

I know it may be a painful sort of favor. It can also be an inconvenient favor. But when God is trying to get you and me to live with the kingdom value of being poor in spirit, it is a divine favor. Because once we know enough to declare spiritual bankruptcy, He opens His storehouses of provision to meet us where we need Him most.

Reaction: In your own words, what does it mean to be poor in spirit?

What would you hope is the outcome of living a life that is truly poor in spirit?

Describe why you believe God would want His followers to live with a heart that is poor in spirit.

Prayer: Jesus, help me have a heart that honors You by being poor in spirit. Reveal to me those areas where I am proud. Show me my own self-

sufficiency so that I can be convicted by what I see and recognize how useless it is to count on myself when I have You to depend on. Bless me in ways that I can recognize are truly from You so that I can learn the power of being poor in spirit. In Your name I pray, amen.

Twenty-Two

For though I caused you sorrow by my letter, I do not regret it; though I did regret it—for I see that that letter caused you sorrow, though only for a while—I now rejoice, not that you were made sorrowful, but that you were made sorrowful to the point of repentance; for you were made sorrowful according to the will of God, so that you might not suffer loss in anything through us. For the sorrow that is according to the will of God produces a repentance without regret, leading to salvation, but the sorrow of the world produces death.

2 Corinthians 7:8–10

Anyone who has grieved knows the toll it can take on your ability to think clearly, function fully, and even get through some days. I'm fairly certain no one considers mourning a positive thing. Most of us live with the hope that we can somehow avoid it. But Jesus spoke of this process in a whole new way. He addressed our well-known, and often well-avoided, emotion of mourning by connecting it to something different than we may expect when we hear the term.

We read in the Sermon on the Mount that Jesus said, "Blessed are those who mourn, for they shall be comforted" (Matthew 5:4). If we were to change this statement into terms we often use today, it might say, "Blessed are those who are sad or despondent, for they will be comforted." In whatever ways we change the terms, though, most people hearing it would still be confused as to how *blessed* and *mourning* or *sadness* or even *despondency* can show up together in the same sentence.

After all, we live in a fun, entertainment-based culture. Most of us want to plow through any amount of grief or sadness that we experience. We prefer to get through it quickly so that we don't have to experience it for any length of time. This is because in our society, laughter is what is loved. Excitement is what is emphasized. And any form of sorrow is often sought to be medicated right away. Enjoyment has become one of our premiere idols.

And yet, Jesus says we are blessed if we cry. We are comforted when we grieve. We gain spiritually when we mourn.

But how can that be? If we read His statement without further study, it could leave us confused. It could create a mental daze because it is such an exact opposite of what our culture pushes and seeks to inspire. Because of that, many of us simply skip over this portion of His sermon on kingdom values, similar to how we seek to skip past any process of grief or mourning.

What I want to do is encourage us to look at it more closely. Because when we look at the contextual environment of the culture in which Jesus spoke, we find a lot more to this verse than meets the eye.

Second Corinthians 7:8–10 gives this greater insight into the full meaning of mourning during the days when Jesus walked on earth. To mourn doesn't only refer to grieving the loss of a loved one, as we often associate it with today. Neither does it only refer to grieving the loss of a dream, or a way of life, or a relationship. To mourn something involves feeling sorrow over it.

It could be compared to what many people went through when the pandemic hit. Many of us grieved the loss of what we once depended on as "normalcy" and even "predictability." We probably wouldn't call it mourning, but those are the feelings many experienced at the sudden changes. Weddings were postponed, vacations cancelled, family birthday parties prevented from taking place like they used to. Each of these losses stacked up on each other and created a grief we felt inside.

A lot of times these feelings were referred to as "social isolation depression," but essentially, we mourned. We grieved the loss of routine. Mourning and grief can surround many things in our lives, not just the death of a loved one.

Reaction: What are some things you are mourning in your present situation?

What have some of the outcomes been from this experience of mourning?

Describe any benefits that mourning can bring to a believer's life.

Prayer: *Jesus, it's easy to seek fun and entertainment because these things often distract us from emotions we may not want to feel. Yet the emotions of mourning and grief produce spiritual gain when we acknowledge them and allow them to do their work in our lives. I praise You and thank You for the opportunities I have to mourn because I know these opportunities can bring me closer to You and Your will for my life if I respond to them spiritually. In Your name, amen.*

Twenty-Three

"Blessed are those who mourn, for they shall be comforted."

Matthew 5:4

In the Bible, there is only one thing a person repents from, and that is sin. In the passage in 2 Corinthians we looked at yesterday, Paul speaks of a sorrow related to the presence of sin in the life of a believer. Essentially, he states that those who are sad over the presence of sin operating in their lives will be blessed. Blessed are those who are sad to the point of going to God and repenting because of the presence and impact of sin in their lives.

Worldly sorrow comes tied to the consequences of sin in a person's life. This occurs whether a person is a Christian or not. Nobody wants the negative repercussions that come from bad decisions. That's a natural sorrow that anyone feels when they have to pay the piper for the wrong choices they've made. But that's not the kind of sorrow Paul speaks about.

Paul speaks of a sorrow not created by consequences. Rather, he speaks of a sorrow created by the cause itself. In other words, the sorrow he writes on relates more to the sin that caused the consequences and simultaneously saddened the heart of God. This is the sorrow, or mourning, he reflects on. And this is the sorrow that can bring about a blessing in a person's life.

An important thing we need to understand about God is that one of His chief attributes and characteristics is holiness. He is distinctly holy. *Holiness* means to "be set apart." God exists separate from sin. Sin, to God, is similar to rotten garbage to us. No one would want to live in an environment of rotten, smelly garbage and seek to stay there. It isn't a good experience. It wouldn't be pleasant. Nearly everyone, if not everyone, would be unhappy to hang out with garbage because garbage smells. It has a stench to it. If it were piled up in your home in every room, you would either get rid of it or go look for another place to live. Because living with the stench of garbage, as well as what rotten garbage attracts—rats, ants, flies, maggots, and more— would prove to be unsanitary and a health hazard. It's unacceptable.

That's why we take our garbage out, where it gets picked up and delivered to a garbage collection location and dealt with. Or, if you live in a location that doesn't have garbage pickup, you probably have a garbage pit where you burn it and bury it over time. If you are a parent, you have probably urged your kid or kids to clean their room because you don't want them living in a room with a mess or garbage. None of us takes any delight in hanging out with garbage, whether it's our own or someone else's.

But when sin is operating in the life of a believer, he or she is asking a holy God to hang out with garbage. They are saying that even though they know that Christ lives in them in the presence of the Holy Spirit, they aren't going to address or remove the filth of sin in their lives. Basically, they are telling God to get used to the smell.

When Jesus gave us the kingdom value of mourning, He was telling us that we were blessed when we have inner anguish over the garbage we've allowed in our lives. We are blessed when we mourn the garbage allowed in the world. We are blessed when we experience sadness for the sinful garbage present in the lives of those we love and fellow believers in Christ. Blessed is the one who is not comfortable with their own or this world's contaminated garbage.

Reaction: What "garbage" needs to be taken out in your life?

Have you ever taken out "garbage" in your spiritual life and experienced God's blessing as a result? If yes, describe what you learned from that time.

In what ways does the culture seek to make people comfortable with hoarding their "garbage" and spiritual sins?

Prayer: *Jesus, I do not want to live a life of sin. I want to be clean from sin's contaminants in my life. I confess my sin to You and pray that You will forgive me of my sin and ungodliness. Cleanse me so that I will be clean and holy before God. In Your name I pray, amen.*

Twenty-Four

When I kept silent about my sin, my body wasted
   away
Through my groaning all day long.
For day and night Your hand was heavy upon me;
My vitality was drained away as with the fever heat
   of summer. *Selah.*
I acknowledged my sin to You,
And my iniquity I did not hide;
I said, "I will confess my transgressions to the LORD";
And You forgave the guilt of my sin.

Psalm 32:3–5

Our culture places fun and pleasure on a pedestal.
Many times, those two things are the goal in advertise-
ments and entertainment. Because of this, we often get
a skewed view of the spiritual kingdom value known
as mourning. In Ecclesiastes 7:2, the Bible says that
a funeral is better than a party. This is because at a
funeral you will be guided to think about what really
matters. You will be guided to make wiser choices in
the life you still have on earth. A party merely camou-
flages what truly matters. But a funeral forces you to
think, evaluate, and consider how you are choosing to
spend your time.

Similarly, Jesus says we need to think, evaluate, and consider how we choose to spend our time when it comes to sin and poor choices in our lives. Do we dismiss what we have done or thought? Do we hide it? Do we continue in it? Or do we recognize the damage it creates and acknowledge it so that we will turn from it? The psalmist David wrote about sin's lasting impact on a soul in Psalm 32, which we read in today's opening Scripture.

David told us that as long as he didn't deal with his sin, he lived in a restless state. Yet when he dealt with it biblically—when he repented (confessed and turned away)—all the pain and anguish he was experiencing due to his sin went away. You and I are blessed when we recognize our own sin, and when we recognize what it does to the heart of God. We are blessed when we respond by confessing and repenting of our sin so that we can have restored fellowship with God.

I know that it hurts to mourn. Trust me, I know. But what Jesus assures us in this kingdom value is that if we choose to mourn and grieve over our sin and its impact on our relationship with God, we will be comforted. We will be forgiven. We will be blessed. On the other hand, refusal to address our sin blocks our prayers from being heard and answered (Psalm 66:18).

You go to a doctor when you're in pain. You go to the doctor to tell him or her what's wrong. You go with the hope that they will know what to do to bring you comfort and restored well-being. You want the doctor to turn things around. Choosing to live according to this kingdom value is no different. Blessed are those who realize they are in spiritual pain because of sin, and so they go to God to restore their well-being.

The prodigal son received comfort by the father when he came home. He received forgiveness. One of the reasons is because he returned to his father repentant for what he had done wrong. He didn't return bragging about his disobedience and hardened by it. He returned in a state of humility and was blessed by his father as a result.

Jesus says that you will also be blessed with the comfort and love of God when you return to Him in a state of humility and mourning over your sin. You will find the comfort you need to navigate the chaos around you when you choose to call sin what it is—sin. You will find comfort when you respond to it with the anguish of a heart that seeks to honor God in all you do.

Reaction: Describe what it means to you to experience God's comfort in your life.

Do you feel like you are living more in a state of restlessness or in a state of experiencing God's comfort?

In what ways can you better position yourself spiritually so that you tap in to God's comfort?

Prayer: *Jesus, help me to experience God's comfort at a greater level in my life by being more honest about my sinful thoughts and actions and repenting of them. Help me evaluate my choices in light of Your kingdom values, as well as in light of eternity. Show me what I can do differently to live a purer life. Let Your love and purity surround me to such a degree that I feel it and want to seek to model You in all I do. In Your name, amen.*

Twenty-Five

> For the wrath of God is revealed from heaven against all ungodliness and unrighteousness of men who suppress the truth in unrighteousness, because that which is known about God is evident within them; for God made it evident to them. For since the creation of the world His invisible attributes, His eternal power and divine nature, have been clearly seen, being understood through what has been made, so that they are without excuse.
>
> Romans 1:18–20

One of my all-time favorite movies is *A Few Good Men*. Most people who have seen the film remember the epic scene as the movie rolls to its conclusion. Tom Cruise's character is interrogating Jack Nicholson's character on the stand. They intently stare each other down as their passions rise. Tom Cruise's character then pounds firmly on the table as he yells, "I want the truth!"

That's when Jack Nicholson looks him in the eye and snaps back, "You can't handle the truth!"

It seems that is where we have landed in our culture today. Everybody claims that they want truth in some form or fashion. But when truth comes to the surface, most people can't handle it. That's why a call for truth becomes little more than a call for consensus these days. It is a call for what the culture or the ruling in-fluencers will deem is true—until it changes directions, and another call for consensus goes out.

The problem is, truth isn't created by consensus, and what's more, its removal comes with consequences. If and when a culture chooses to suppress truth, that culture will face the consequences of its own choices. This is because you can't be both "poor in spirit" and think you are the author of what is true. Pride is the backing of the "your truth" and "my truth" movement. Anytime we sidestep and marginalize God's truth, we have leaned into pride. God opposes all forms of pride, and He meets it with His wrath.

The reason God's wrath rains down can be found in Romans 1:18–20. Essentially, the blame is on us. We read that God unleashes His wrath "because that which is known about God is evident within them; for God made it evident to them" (v. 19). To put it like a parent: we should know better than that. God has made truth evident to us. To suppress it is to deny its reality.

Everyone is born with a conscience. We have been given a truth-regulator—a smoke detector of the soul. Our conscience knows the truth. Similarly, our conscience knows the smoke and mirrors of a lie. That's why you have probably found yourself innately knowing when something or someone is wrong, or off, or shady. You know this because you are built with a conscience tied to truth.

The suppression of truth, in time, warps the conscience. It dulls the conscience. Like batteries wearing out in the smoke detector, the conscience becomes less and less activated or alert. Before you know it, a person's conscience can be buried so deep under a pile of lies that the person can no longer distinguish between truth and fiction, right and wrong. This is because the conscience has become dulled and calloused. It no longer works, with the result that it destroys the character of a person or a group of people.

Reaction: What is your personal definition of *pride*?

Why do you think God opposes pride?

What do you think is God's definition of *truth*?

Prayer: Jesus, help me walk in Your truth and not give in to the pride seeking to compete with You that wells up within me. I humble myself before You and ask that You will reveal to me the steps I am to take in order to glorify You and make You known. I love You and want my life to reflect Your love to others. In Your name, amen.

Twenty-Six

"Blessed are the gentle, for they shall inherit the earth."

Matthew 5:5

One of the greatest kingdom virtues is gentleness. However, many people have a wrong definition of what *gentleness* means. Gentleness does not mean to make yourself a pushover. Neither does it mean to become a wallflower. Instead, gentleness involves strength. It involves the wisdom of how to use your strength strategically. Gentleness is actually strength that is directed for a good use while under control. For example, when you are watering your plants in your backyard, it's the difference between spraying a water hose with the spout wide open or directing the water into a single funnel. The pressure from the water is the same, but the power from the directed funnel is more effective for reaching plants or bushes farther away. This saves you steps in the long run as well.

When Jesus urged His followers to live a meek and gentle life, saying that doing so would bring about blessings (Matthew 5:5), He said this at a time when the Jews were under Roman domination. He said this to a group of people who wanted to rise up in full force to topple those who oppressed them. The Jews were being oppressed and wanted nothing more than to get the Romans off their backs. They wanted freedom from the stranglehold of Roman rule, and because of it, they were looking for a leader who would set them free. Thus, Jesus offered them an effective strategy contrary to what they could think up on their own.

The Greek word for meek or gentle is *praos*. It describes the necessary balance between using power and avoiding harshness. It was a term typically used of domesticated animals. If you've been to a circus, you know what this looks like with some of the strongest animals around, such as tigers and bears, or even elephants. When a professional trains one of these animals, they do not strip the animal of its power. Rather, they instruct the animal on how to contain its power in certain scenarios.

The concept of gentleness never refers to the loss of strength, like Superman in the presence of kryptonite. Gentleness refers to taming power so that it can be surrendered to the overall goals at hand. If you have ever seen a wild stallion that has been broken, you have witnessed meekness. The broken horse has not lost its power. Rather, the horse's power is now harnessed under the control and guidance of the rider who directs it where it needs to go.

When you do this, you no longer have to try to force things to go as you hoped. You can yield the outcomes to God, who is far stronger and more capable than you, and allow Him the freedom to work things out for you. Far too many of us actually get in the way of God showing up and working things out in our lives because we lack this virtue of self-control. We feel like we have to figure things out. We have to solve things. We have to muscle our way through. We have to let our voices be heard. Whatever the issues are that we are facing, we often get in the way of God intervening on our behalf because we are seeking our own way rather than His way. But living with the value of gentleness opens the door for God's power to work for us and through us for His glory.

One of the most exciting things in life is to watch God work stuff out for you when you didn't have any idea how it could possibly work out at all. There's nothing quite like that experience. But that is not an experience everyone gets to have. That experience belongs to the meek. It belongs to the gentle. It belongs to those who humble themselves under God and align their lives under His rule. It is reserved for those who are committed to Christ and the will of God.

Reaction: What does the word *gentleness* mean to you?

Describe how you feel about living your life in a spirit of ongoing gentleness.

Is there a part of you that feels afraid to live with a spirit of ongoing gentleness? If so, describe those emotions and try to identify why they might be there.

Prayer: Jesus, show me how to find the courage to live with gentleness rather than seeking to solve my own problems through my own strength unleashed. Give me opportunities to experience the strength of gentleness working on my behalf so I will gain greater confidence in it as a kingdom virtue. Help my thoughts and actions to always honor You in everything that I do. I pray this in Your name, amen.

Twenty-Seven

Seek the LORD,
All you humble of the earth
Who have carried out His ordinances;
Seek righteousness, seek humility.
Perhaps you will be hidden
In the day of the LORD's anger.

Zephaniah 2:3

If you visit a dentist, my guess is that you would want your dentist to be gentle. No one I know says they look forward to finding a rough or abrasive dentist. Everyone wants a gentle dentist. In fact, dentists know this and will often name their practice with the word *gentle* in it somehow to express to patients this is a high value for them.

Now, if you visit a dentist, you also don't want a dentist who is weak. You don't want a fearful, hesitant, or fly-on-the-wall type of dentist. Of course, you want a dentist with confidence, courage, and inner strength. The reason is because you will get better treatment when your dentist has those character qualities. This is a perfect example of what gentleness is as a kingdom value. It is not the removal of confidence, courage, or inner strength. Rather, it is the focusing of those traits into a strategic delivery format that is most easily received by those around you.

Any man or woman who cannot tame themselves is out of control. Their lives will be earmarked by chaos, because if you cannot bring your own thoughts, words, and actions into alignment with overarching goals, then you will not be able to live up to your fullest potential. You can identify someone who lacks basic character qualities, especially meekness, because they are a person who loses control. They become angry quickly. They mouth off easily. They get irritated at other drivers or other people posting on social media, or even throw things at the TV. The chaos they put out simply reflects the chaos within.

Gentleness, which comes from having a humble heart, is such an important value to live by that Proverbs 25:28 compares a lack of it to a city about to be overrun by its enemy: "Like a city that is broken into and without walls is a man who has no control over his spirit." As we see in today's verse, Zephaniah 2:3, we are to set out intentionally to seek to have more humility. According to Zephaniah, we are not to just be humble and gentle, but we are also to seek this trait. He is writing to those who are already known as the "humble of the earth." Yet he tells them to seek more humility, warning them that it will be a shield of protection for them.

Regardless of strength, skill, power, education, financial wealth, or anything else—it is humility that identifies a person in God's eyes as great. God opposes pride in people because pride dismisses God's hand of work and His rule over all. If you want to experience God's provision and power made manifest in your life, then coming under Him and His rule in a spirit of gentleness is key. It is in living according to this kingdom value that you will learn how to focus your strength and use it in effective ways, rather than unleashing it in catastrophic ways.

God created each of us to live out a personal calling and destiny. Sometimes when we get a vision of what our personal calling or destiny is, we aim to fulfill it on our own and in our own strength. When we bump into obstacles, rather than looking to God with a heart of humility, we take the attitude that since it's our destiny, we need to overcome the obstacles our way. Living with a heart of gentleness will be a constant reminder that muscling through the mess of life is never the right approach. Living with a spirit of gentleness will enable you to look to God to help you overcome any and every obstacle in your way, and then thank Him for what He has done both in you and through you. This kingdom value known as gentleness is a precursor to a heart of gratitude. When you have both, you will be positioning yourself to become truly great in the kingdom of God.

Reaction: Describe the difference between unleashing chaotic strength and focused or targeted strength.

In what areas do you feel you could improve when it comes to being more gentle?

Why does God want you to live with a spirit of gentleness?

Prayer: *Jesus, to be gentle is not to remove my strength from practice, but rather to target it. Help me understand that truth internally so that I will apply this kingdom value more in my life. Show me other people who practice this kingdom value of humility and gentleness very well so I can see examples to model after from a practical standpoint. Thank You. In Your name I pray, amen.*

Twenty-Eight

Therefore, putting aside all filthiness and all that remains of wickedness, in humility receive the word implanted, which is able to save your souls.

James 1:21

The kingdom value of gentleness has nothing to do with submitting to anyone and everyone around you. It has to do with yielding to the legitimate authority who is ultimately over you, which is God. It is seeking to align all you think, do, and say under the overarching rule of God in every area of your life.

One of the greatest challenges I have when it comes to counseling people as their pastor is the overwhelming number who seem unwilling to submit to God's spiritual authority. They may not want to give up premarital sex. Or getting drunk. Or pornography. I can explain the biblical principles on whatever area they are facing, but if they are not willing to apply those spiritual principles personally, there is no impact. Once a person chooses to live with a rebellious spirit, that person has also chosen to cancel the work of God in their lives.

Now, the term *rebellious spirit* may seem strong to you. Perhaps you don't consider making decisions outside of the rule of God as rebellion. Maybe you look at it like independence or even personal wisdom. But whenever someone chooses their own way over God's way, it is known as rebellion to God. It is living with the idea or concept that you know better than the God who made you and who also made the universe in which you live. The only thing that could lead to thinking that way is personal pride. Personal wisdom is personal pride if it does not align under God's overarching rule.

Pride can only be present in the absence of humility and gentleness. The absence of humility and gentleness brings chaos. But the presence of humility and gentleness to God brings calm. In fact, it'll bring calm to such a degree that it is able to "save" or "sanctify" individuals in the midst of personal life struggles (James 1:21).

A gentle person bows low before God so that he or she can stand tall among people. It is in an individual's willingness to bow before God where the greatest power can be found. The largest players on any football team are the offensive linemen. They are the biggest, strongest, and fiercest. But if you'll notice, they are also the ones who have to go the lowest when it's time to run a play. The reason why they go so low and dig their knuckles into the ground is for leverage. It is in doing so that they access their power.

Similarly, when you bow before God in humility, you will discover your greatest spiritual leverage and strength. You will be able to spot the opponent's tactics more easily than ever before. You will be able to tackle the enemy in the power and might of Christ. This is God's revealed will for you. You are to live as someone who overwhelmingly conquers in Jesus' name. But you only do this through a heart that is willing to go low through surrender and humility before God.

Living with a heart of gentleness is the fastest way to finding out what true strength looks like. That statement may seem contrary to anything you might believe or think, but that is why God asks us to walk by faith and not by our own human logic. Faith is God's love language. Walking by faith in what He reveals to be true allows you to experience His power in your life. You will see Him do things both in you and through you that you never even dreamed possible.

Reaction: Describe the difference between personal wisdom rooted in your own thoughts and godly wisdom.

Define *rebellion* in your own terms.

What is one thing you can do to cultivate the kingdom value of gentleness in your life to a higher degree?

Prayer: Jesus, my relationship to You rests in humility. You are my Savior, and You rule over all. Forgive me for those times when pride raises its head within me and seeks to take over my thoughts and actions. Forgive me for living in rebellion to You in those times when I have done just that. Help me honor You with a heart of humility. In Your name, amen.

Twenty-Nine

Rest in the LORD and wait patiently for Him;
Do not fret because of him who prospers in his way,
Because of the man who carries out wicked
    schemes.
Cease from anger and forsake wrath;
Do not fret; it leads only to evildoing.
For evildoers will be cut off,
But those who wait for the LORD, they will inherit the
    land.
Yet a little while and the wicked man will be no
    more;
And you will look carefully for his place and he will
    not be there.
But the humble will inherit the land
And will delight themselves in abundant prosperity.

Psalm 37:7–11

The Hoover Dam produces enough energy for California, Nevada, and Arizona. It is concentrated power under control. Because of this, it can produce enough for all three states. But if you ever loose that water, it would bring disaster to the very areas it was designed to help. When power exists without control, it's a tsunami. It's a flood. It's a torrent of chaos sweeping over and through the land, destroying all life in its way.

We've all seen people on the news or elsewhere who seem to have lost all sense of control. It's enough to make you think they must have gone crazy. They are doing things that are unconscionable. This is because they have lost the ability to control their own life-force—the power they have within them.

As we've been reviewing in the last few devotionals, living with the value of gentleness translates into living with the value of self-control. You cannot have one without the other. When you and I surrender our lives to Jesus Christ, we are to surrender our gifts, skills, talents, and personal strength under the authority of God.

Most of the chaos we are facing today in homes, communities, churches, and in our culture is simply due to a lack of self-control. Personal surrender to the legitimate authority of God's rule is the key to living out the fullness of your destiny.

I want you to remember that meekness is never translated as weakness. Uncontrolled passions, un-inhibited desires, and all forms of sin are weakness. Sin brings about terrible consequences in a person's life. Humility and surrender bring about blessing. As we saw in a previous day's Scripture reading of Matthew 5:5, "Blessed are the gentle, for they shall inherit the earth." We discover more about what it means to inherit the earth when we look at another passage found in Psalm 37. Sprinkled throughout this psalm are references to inheriting the earth or receiving the blessing of God's provision.

The psalmist begins by warning us not to become frustrated or upset when we see evil people flourish. He writes, "Do not fret because of evildoers, be not envious toward wrongdoers. For they will wither quickly like the grass and fade like the green herb" (vv. 1–2). In the beginning of this passage, we are reminded that what we see physically taking place isn't always God's endgame. It's a step in the process where God ultimately defeats evil. Those who learn how to remain self-controlled and live according to His kingdom values will experience a greater provision of His intended blessings in our lives as He carries out His will on earth.

Reaction: What thoughts go through your head when you see people who are clearly living outside the will of God, prospering by the world's standards?

Have you witnessed someone living outside God's will be brought to a place of humility? If yes, what did you learn by witnessing this?

How can we encourage others in our lives to live in a spirit of gentleness?

Prayer: *Jesus, Your prescribed kingdom values are there to help us so that we can enjoy Your blessings and benefits and be free from the consequences of our own sins. Help me not react to those around me whom I see prospering outside of Your prescribed kingdom values, but rather let me trust in Your Word found in Psalm 37. I want to stay in alignment under You and not be caught up in my own emotional reactions that take me outside Your will. In Your name I pray, amen.*

Thirty

"Blessed are those who hunger and thirst for righteousness, for they shall be satisfied."

Matthew 5:6

Have you ever been so hungry you could hardly think straight? Some people refer to this as being "hangry." It's when your personality changes to that of anger rather than calm, simply due to being hungry. Hunger is an important feeling because it is a signal that we need to eat. Our body needs fuel. Hunger typically propels us to do something about it. It's not something you can easily ignore for any length of time.

That's why in trying to create a mental correlation we can understand quickly, Jesus used the reference of hunger for the next kingdom value we are looking at. He said we are blessed when we are hungry and thirsty. Now, He didn't mean when we hunger and thirst for food and drink. Rather, He said, "Blessed are those who hunger and thirst for righteousness, for they shall be satisfied" (Matthew 5:6).

Those who live with the kingdom value of desire for God's ways, His rules, and His righteous standards will experience satisfied lives.

Appetite is one of the great indicators to a doctor of your health. Consistent loss of appetite is an indication of a much deeper problem. That's why one of the first questions a nurse or a doctor will ask when you go in for a visit is how your appetite has been. Similarly, spiritual appetite is one of the great indicators to God of your spiritual health. If you experience no appetite for Him and His truth or values, then you are revealing a lack of need and connection to Him. This particular kingdom value is easy to spot. The idiomatic expression of "hunger and thirst" shows up as a passionate desire propelled by heavy longing. It produces actions that are recognizable.

While we all have felt hunger from time to time, it's true that we live in a day when most of us don't have to worry about being hungry for very long. The access to food in the Western world is replete. Sure, we may be inconvenienced by the time it takes to go to a store or restaurant, but very few of us in our nation know true physical hunger.

It wasn't like that in biblical days when there were no freezers or refrigerators. People had to hustle after food day in, day out because it couldn't typically be preserved for extended periods of time. In addition, food preparation was often laborious and lengthy. People didn't necessarily snack all day like so many have become accustomed to in modern nations. They couldn't just wake up in the middle of the night and go to the refrigerator or pantry for a quick snack. Meals had designated times. Leftovers didn't last long. Either due to consumption, rot, or a need to be used for livestock or another purpose, not much food would have been wasted. Little is wasted when little is all you've got.

Many who lived in the day and age in which Jesus spoke these words knew exactly what it was like to feel hungry. They knew what it was like to be thirsty. They knew what it was like to have gone an extended amount of time without the nourishment they needed.

Real hunger can be so deep and so gnawing that it can literally hurt, keeping someone awake all night. This is the hunger and the thirst Jesus spoke about. This is how we are to feel toward obtaining righteousness in our lives.

Reaction: Describe a moment in your life when you were so hungry that it affected what you could do or think about.

What did you choose to do about it?

What can this experience teach you about the level of hunger you are to have for righteousness?

Prayer: Jesus, You have taught us that we are to hunger and thirst for righteousness, so I want to do this in such a way that pleases You. Help me gain a better understanding of what this means and what this looks like in my life. In Your name I pray, amen.

Thirty-One

He who walks righteously and speaks with sincerity,
He who rejects unjust gain
And shakes his hands so that they hold no bribe;
He who stops his ears from hearing about bloodshed
And shuts his eyes from looking upon evil;
He will dwell on the heights,
His refuge will be the impregnable rock;
His bread will be given him,
His water will be sure.

Your eyes will see the King in His beauty;
They will behold a far-distant land.

Isaiah 33:15–17

There exists one common trait that shows up among the great people of Scripture and that is their hunger and thirst after God. In some form or fashion, they have a passionate pursuit of God. They are on fire to find Him and to experience Him at a deeper level. Like Moses, the longing cry of their hearts echoes his "show me Your glory!" (Exodus 33:18).

One of the reasons so many of us experience so little of God is that so many of us are not hungry. Hungry people are going to do everything in their power to locate some food. Hungry people are going to think of little else than finding food. Hungry and thirsty people are going to remove distractions and cut short diversions so that they can find something to eat or drink. This is because they are desperate for something that will satisfy. They crave it. They need it. They long for it.

One of the ways I often travel when I'm on the East Coast is by train, particularly if I am traveling between major cities. I'll just get on a train, and in a few hours, or even less, I'll be at my destination. If you've ever gotten on a train anywhere, you have probably noticed, like I have, that the cost of food does not reflect the cost of food elsewhere. You have probably noticed that on a train, they will charge you an unconscionable amount just to sell you something to eat. You can literally pay ten dollars for a hot dog, or eight dollars for a soda. You might even pay five dollars just for a small bag of chips.

Now, the reason they have chosen to charge you so much on a train is that they know you can't go anywhere else. They know you have no other options. No one is going to hop off the train in order to grab a meal and then hop back on. Theirs is the only gig in town, so they price themselves like the only gig in town.

Sure, passengers may say that they simply won't pay that much on a train, and they won't support such an extortion-based business model. But that really depends on how hungry they are, or how hungry they get as the train keeps moving on. Because if they get hungry enough, in time, neither the price tag nor their principles will prohibit them from pursuing the food they want.

My mom used to tell me and my siblings if we complained about something she was cooking, and we didn't want to eat it, that we just weren't hungry enough. We would excuse ourselves from the table and head elsewhere in the house only to hear her say, "You'll be back. When you get hungry enough, it'll be here." This is because my mom knew, like many moms know, that hungry people who are truly hungry aren't that picky. They just need food. And they won't let their own preferences keep them from pursuing the nutrition and sustenance that will satisfy their bodies' needs.

Most Christians just want appetizers. They only want to nibble on spiritual food. It used to be that Sunday sermons might be an entire meal that a lot of Christians would try and survive on for the rest of the week. But these days with so much of Sunday worship centered more on Sunday celebrities preaching or singing, you don't even get a meal. You might get a few bites here or there, but it's an appetizer at best. A Sunday meal would never get anyone through the rest of an entire week anyhow, let alone a Sunday appetizer. If someone tried to live like that in the physical realm, they would be dead by the next Sunday. Nourishment requires consistency.

When Jesus speaks of our kingdom values involving a passionate pursuit of righteousness, He is speaking of an ongoing prioritization of the pursuit of righteousness.

Reaction: In what ways do you tend to put off the pursuit of righteousness, thinking you'll just return to God when you're really "hungry"?

In what ways can you become more consistent and persistent in your pursuit of righteousness?

What are some hopeful benefits you would like to see show up in your life as a result of pursuing righteousness?

Prayer: *Jesus, slow down my activities to a more manageable pace that will enable me to recognize room for pursuing righteousness. Increase my hunger for holiness and modeling my life after You. Reveal to me what is true righteousness and what is merely a charade. I want to live in the fullness of Your blessings and favor. In Your name I pray, amen.*

Thirty-Two

"Why do you spend money for what is not bread,
And your wages for what does not satisfy?
Listen carefully to Me, and eat what is good,
And delight yourself in abundance."

Isaiah 55:2

The spiritual life demands righteousness in order to function as it was designed to function. Your physical being has a design, which includes needing food. Your spiritual being has a design that includes needing righteousness. The Bible calls the spiritual being the "divine nature." Righteousness is the nutrients God provides for your divine nature.

Righteousness isn't just an ethereal term referring to some intangible halo hovering over certain people. Righteousness is very real. It involves making choices on a regular basis that promote your living in accordance with God's will. It can be described as "right living." It includes identifying God's will on a matter and seeking to line up your life in accordance with it. To put it simply, it means aligning according to God's kingdom rule.

The problems come when people search after illegitimate food to feed a legitimate spiritual need for righteousness. This search can include many different things. It can include seeking after self-help gurus, or any number of things. While these are not bad in and of themselves, if they are sought after to a degree as to replace the righteousness of God in your life, that is when they become bad.

Enjoying cake is one thing. Seeking to satisfy the needs of the body with cake is another. Most of us understand that. But when it comes to spiritual nourishment, that truth gets lost. Far too many believers today seek for that which "is not bread," and they waste their money on that which "does not satisfy." Only a deceived person would believe that eating cake every day as your only source of food would address what the body is calling for. Likewise, only a deceived person would believe that spiritual nourishment is sustained by listening to a sermon once a week, or reading a few verses of the Bible, or saying a prayer before they eat.

Cake is fundamentally empty calories. While it may give you a semblance of satisfaction for an immediate period of time, it will not provide lasting nutrition. Cake is not designed to feed the cellular structure of the human body. It may be enjoyable, but it does not satisfy long-term. It does not have staying power. In fact, a lot of people will become even more hungry after eating cake because the sugar and carbs stimulate the brain to crave more food. Thus, it starts a cycle of feeding that is sometimes difficult to stop. When you and I try to nourish our divine nature with that which is not bread and that which does not satisfy, we wind up starving to spiritual death, all the while craving more of the world's ways.

Satan is very clever on how he seeks to deceive believers into thinking they are truly consuming spiritual food and righteousness. The Bible says one way he does this is through spiritual teachers who only deliver messages that aim to "tickle the ears" of the hearers (see 2 Timothy 4:3). But tickling your ears spiritually does not translate into hungering and thirsting after righteousness. That translates more into entertainment. Satan doesn't mind if religious sayings or speakers entertain you at all. The reason is because he knows there is no power in religious entertainment. The power comes through tapping in to spiritual authority, which can only be done by aligning your heart, thoughts, words, and actions under the truth of God's Word. That is what it means to hunger after righteousness. It is to feed on that which is true and apply it to your life on a regular basis.

Reaction: Why doesn't simply listening to a fun, entertaining sermon equip you as a believer to stand against Satan's schemes?

What are some elements of righteous living that do not often show up in messages or books merely meant to "tickle the ears"?

Name one way you can encourage others to pursue righteousness consistently in their lives.

Prayer : *Jesus, I want to honor You by encouraging others to live righteous lives. Show me how to do that in a way that is winsome and impactful to them. Open the doors for me to be a greater example of someone who seeks after righteousness and lives in a right relationship with You. I pray this in Your name, amen.*

Thirty-Three

> Now flee from youthful lusts and pursue righteousness, faith, love and peace, with those who call on the Lord from a pure heart.
>
> 2 Timothy 2:22

Though you may go to church or you even do religious activities, if you are not hungering and thirsting after what your soul truly needs, you will starve spiritually. In order for your soul to flourish, it requires a consistent feeding of righteousness. The soul is nourished when you align yourself in accordance with the truth of God.

For example, if you were to go fill up your car with diesel fuel when it requires unleaded, you would be in for a rough ride, and you wouldn't get very far. It doesn't matter how new your car is. It doesn't matter how much money you put into your car. If you put diesel fuel in an unleaded car's motor, you'll ruin it. This is because your car's motor is not designed to receive diesel.

It won't even matter how much diesel you put in it or if your gas tank registers as completely full. You will simply sputter down the road until you stop. You have to put unleaded fuel into a car designed to run on unleaded fuel. That's not too difficult for most of us to comprehend. And yet many of us are confused when we put all of the world's junk and all the culture's chaotic stuff into our souls and then wonder why we sputter through life and don't get very far.

We can't make it on the world's fuel because our divine nature—that which empowers our spiritual being—requires righteousness based on truth. We run smoothly when we align our thoughts, decisions, and words under the overarching rule of God in our life. Anything else will cause problems under the hood of our souls. We can go to church on Sunday or even have daily devotions, but if we're not obeying God, it won't mean much. Are you listening to Him when it comes to your sex life? Your finances? Your temper?

From time to time when I am scheduled to preach, I'll look out into the audience during a song or some other part of the service. Without fail, I'll see a mother with a baby in her arms. Now, particularly if the baby is young, she may sit toward the back so that she can get to one of the cry rooms if the baby starts fussing. But normally the mother will try to console the baby with a pacifier first. The problems come when the baby realizes that the pacifier is fake food. It's a piece of rubber designed to trick a kid. Despite how much the baby sucks on the pacifier, the baby won't be receiving any nourishment at all.

After a while, the baby will let out a loud cry because the baby knows he or she has been fooled. If the baby could talk, you might hear something like, "Mama, you're playing with my emotions!" That's when the mom will get up and go to the cry room to feed the baby. A baby can only be pacified with fake food for so long. If the hunger is strong enough, the entire congregation will hear the cry.

Many people come to church on Sunday and are satisfied with a pacifier-sermon or a pacifier-song because it makes them feel good for a moment. But not too long after the sermon or the song, they will discover they are still hungry. A pacifier is not designed to be the sole source of nourishment. The feeding of the soul demands a consistency in righteousness, or it will go hungry. And when your soul is hungry, your whole life cries out in chaos. When we have enough souls that are hungry or starving, our whole culture cries out in chaos.

Jesus said that you are blessed when you hunger and thirst for the only thing that the soul can digest. When you seek to align your life in accordance with the truth of God, you will be feeding yourself with righteousness. Nothing else you give the soul will satisfy it. No matter how often you try to feed your soul with other things, it will never be satisfied with anything other than what it was designed to consume: righteousness.

Reaction: What are some forms of the world's "pacifiers"?

Do you ever feel like you are using a pacifier rather than pursuing the true nourishment of God's Word? If yes, what is often the result?

What are some hesitations you have toward spending more consistent time in God's Word?

Prayer: *Jesus, help me mature spiritually by pursuing You and Your righteousness on a more regular basis. Help me consume the word of Your truth to such a degree that it becomes second nature to my own thoughts and emotions. In Your name I pray, amen.*

Thirty-Four

Be anxious for nothing, but in everything by prayer and supplication with thanksgiving let your requests be made known to God. And the peace of God, which surpasses all comprehension, will guard your hearts and your minds in Christ Jesus.

Philippians 4:6–7

An article was published not too long ago that said Americans had purchased over three hundred million prescriptions for anxiety or anti-depressants in 2021 alone.* That was a sharp increase from the year before and a definite sign of the times. It is clear people are struggling with mental health as we witness the restlessness all around. One of the reasons indicated was a lack of satisfaction with life as it was. And while there is a place for assistance when you need it, God's Word also provides a way to help with calming your heart and emotions. If you find yourself going through the motions each moment when either nothing makes you happy or you have to conjure up happiness to distract you from your unhappiness, you are not pursuing

* Casey Schwartz, "The Age of Distracti-pression," *New York Times*, July 9, 2022, https://www.nytimes.com/2022/07/09/style/medication-depression-anxiety-adhd.html.

righteousness. I can say that because Jesus promises in His Word that you will be satisfied when you are pursuing righteousness.

Satisfaction is yours for the taking. It's as simple as conforming your thoughts and your actions to the will of God. Much of the disenchantment and despondency we face week after week or month after month is tied to famished souls. If the body of Christ would just stop dining solely on spiritual doughnuts, as pleasant as they may taste and as easy as they go down, we would be able to impact the chaos in our culture and transform it for the glory of God.

But we won't do that until we, as a collective body, determine to be as passionate about the truth of God's Word while we pursue an intimate relationship with Him and the primacy of His rule as we are about everything else we've placed ahead of Him so far. Until we start to reject illegitimate sources of nutrition and replace them with the truth, we will remain ineffective followers, unable to make much of a difference at all.

If the physical body needs to have food intake several times a day just to function, how much more do you think the spiritual being needs righteousness on a regular basis? Our souls are starving because we have relegated our relationship with God and His rule to the status of a social media influencer trying to get us to buy the latest shoes or home goods.

God doesn't just want to influence you. He—as God—is in charge. He is the ultimate Ruler, and He rules over all. In order to rightly align under Him, you will need to consistently feed your soul through the exposure of your mind to righteous thoughts, righteous words, and righteous behavior.

And if you're not used to feeding on so much righteousness at one time, then start where you can. Set down your cell phone and pick up your Bible. Turn off the television and read a book or listen to a podcast on righteous-based principles. Start where you can, and as you continue, you will notice your hunger increasing each day. What used to be five minutes of reading may turn into twenty without your even trying.

As your soul expands with the righteousness of God, your hunger and your thirst will grow, too, in order to meet the growing appetite of your soul.

Reaction: Why do you think there is a growing increase in the number of people depending on outside help for mental wellness?

In what ways can a firm faith in God and His Word help bring calm and satisfaction?

Describe what emotional and mental benefits knowing God has brought to you.

Prayer : Jesus, help me understand what I need to do to live my life in a state of harmony, satisfaction, and peace. Give me a deep desire for Your righteousness as I seek You and Your Word above all else. I love You and want to know You more. In Your name I pray, amen.

Thirty-Five

> "Blessed are the merciful, for they shall receive mercy."
>
> Matthew 5:7

"Lord, have mercy!" It's a phrase many, if not most of us have uttered at some time or another. Sometimes we've said it jokingly. Other times we've said it with full meaning. It is a cry to God for His mercy, help, and intervention in what seems like a deep pit and a dark hole. But did you know that mercy comes tied to your actions? The mercy God extends to you is often tied to your own actions toward others. You can actually increase the level of mercy God shows to you by increasing the level of mercy you show to others. That's why it's such an important part of living the successful kingdom life.

Mercy is all about non-judgment. It involves compassion, kindness, hope, and help. Mercy is so important that Jesus included it in His Sermon on the Mount. He called it out as a foundational kingdom value.

Jesus turned to those who extend care and compassion to others when He pointed out how important mercy truly is. He said, "Blessed are the merciful, for they shall receive mercy" (Matthew 5:7). To understand what it means to live with this value of being merciful, we need to first understand mercy.

Mercy assumes that there is a miserable situation needing relief. Mercy can only show up when there have been circumstances to warrant it. *Mercy* can be defined as compassion for someone in need. It involves reducing, removing, or relieving someone's distress.

Scripture tells us that our salvation is a result of mercy. We read in Titus 3:5, "He saved us, not on the basis of deeds which we have done in righteousness, but according to His mercy, by the washing of regeneration and renewing by the Holy Spirit."

We also see in Ephesians 2:4: "But God, being rich in mercy, because of His great love with which He loved us. . . ." In other words, God is rich in relieving people's pain as well as removing or reducing the weight of distress, discouragement, brokenness, and problems that come our way.

In fact, mercy summarizes God's reaction to our individual misery (Psalm 130:1–8). It involves more than feeling sorry for someone. Anyone can feel sorry for someone but then do nothing about it. Mercy means the sorrow you feel for someone else shows up in your actions. Mercy always involves an action that seeks to reduce or remove the misery that has come about in someone else's life.

Far too often we confuse pity or sympathy with

mercy. Just feeling bad for someone is not showing them mercy. Mercy requires an action you take to show someone you care.

Had God only felt sorry for us in our sin, that would not have helped us out one bit. It is because He acted on the sorrow He felt for the state we were in that we were given the opportunity to live full lives, free from the trappings and consequences of our sins, when we come to Him for His mercy. Adopting this kingdom value reflects God's heart of love and kindness to those around us in a tangible, demonstrable manner.

Reaction: What is one way you have shown someone else mercy?

How have you experienced God's mercy in your own life?

Define in your own terms what it means to "show mercy."

Prayer: *Jesus, I want to be a person who not only experiences God's mercy readily in my life, but who shows others mercy, too. Open my eyes to the needs of those around me, while revealing to me the needs that I can meet with what You have blessed me with. In Your name I pray, amen.*

Thirty-Six

The LORD is good to all,
And His mercies are over all His works.

Psalm 145:9

God's mercy serves as an illustration for how we are to be merciful to others. Mercy isn't contingent on what someone else can do. It doesn't depend on if the other person deserves it, either. If we needed to earn the air we breathe or the sunrise that gives us light that God so mercifully supplies, none of us would be here. Mercy presupposes that the person receiving it is not entitled to what he or she is receiving.

Thus, when you show someone mercy, it's not a favor. It's not a business transaction. It's not quid pro quo. Mercy provides relief from sorrow and pronounces a state of well-being on the recipient, regardless of what they have done up to that point.

There are two common reasons people need mercy. One is due to the debilitating impact of sin in their lives. The other is due to the painful weight of circumstances that have arisen as a result of no fault of their own. Yet regardless of the cause of the suffering, mercy extends relief to those who need it, whether or not you agree with them and what they have done in their lives.

One of the most well-known stories of mercy found in the Bible is the story of the Good Samaritan. You may know this story, but it's worth repeating. A man was walking on the road when he was suddenly beaten up and left broken and wounded. Several so-called spiritual people walked past but showed no mercy to him. They merely saw him and went on their way. But when the Samaritan, a person who was normally racially separate from the Jews, walked by, he felt mercy in his heart for the man in need.

Not only did the Samaritan have to overcome a natural tendency to keep walking and attend to his regular business, but he had to overcome a history of racial segregation and hate. The Jews had been less than kind to the Samaritans in both word and deed. And yet this man showed kindness to the man in need.

God wants us to be like the Good Samaritan. He wants us to set aside our own selfishness and our own pain or historical wounds in order to show kindness and mercy to whoever needs it most. We often use the trauma of the past as an excuse to live angry and bitter lives today, feeling that somehow means we are pursuing justice. Yet God reminds us that true justice shows up when we show mercy. This is because it is only when we overcome the evil of hate in our own hearts by showing mercy to those around us that God is freed up to show us mercy as well. God's mercy is often a prerequisite to His justice.

Mercy isn't always about the other person, although that is a big part of what mercy includes. Mercy is also about fine-tuning the emotions in our own hearts so they reflect the heart of God. It involves our own personal spiritual maturity, so we come to look like Jesus in all we think, say, and do. Jesus didn't have to show us mercy when He hung on the cross for our sins. But it was love that motivated Him to do it. He loved the Father, and He loved us. Similarly, our love for God and our love for others show up when we show mercy to someone in need.

Reaction: Why do you think Jesus used the story of the Good Samaritan to illustrate mercy?

How different would this world be if there were more people showing mercy than fighting for their own rights and revenge?

What steps can you take to distance yourself from the cultural hate and anger so prevalent in our world today, as well as judgment toward other groups of people?

Prayer: *Jesus, free me from the need to always be right or to withhold love from those I do not feel deserve it. Show me what a blessing it is to me when I show mercy to others, especially to those I do not feel deserve it. Help me learn through experience that this is a very good thing to do. I love You and am grateful for the mercy You show me every day. In Your name I pray, amen.*

Thirty-Seven

"Two men went up into the temple to pray, one a Pharisee and the other a tax collector. The Pharisee stood and was praying this to himself: 'God, I thank You that I am not like other people: swindlers, unjust, adulterers, or even like this tax collector. I fast twice a week; I pay tithes of all that I get.' But the tax collector, standing some distance away, was even unwilling to lift up his eyes to heaven, but was beating his breast, saying, 'God, be merciful to me, the sinner!' I tell you, this man went to his house justified rather than the other; for everyone who exalts himself will be humbled, but he who humbles himself will be exalted."

Luke 18:10–14

Have you ever looked around you, similar to what the Pharisee did, and inwardly thanked God that you are not like the others? It's okay to admit it if you have. Admitting it is the first step to repentance and getting right with God. This kind of spirit, which causes us to feel better than others, keeps us distant from God and His mercy for us. You'll notice from the passage that God showed mercy to the man who understood that he needed it.

Mercy is sorely lacking today—whether it is in our words, conversations, or in our actions. Yet Jesus says it is this kingdom value that sets up the boomerang effect in your own life to receive it back. Those who show mercy are the same ones who can expect to get mercy. This kingdom value brings the biblical command to do unto others as you would have them do unto you into clearer view. Because the more mercy you are willing to show to others, the more access to mercy God enables you to have for yourself. And who couldn't use a bit of mercy in their life from time to time? I think we all can.

Showing mercy to others requires that we first adopt the previous kingdom values in our lives, because mercy must be pure in motive for it to be mercy. A prideful person will never show mercy. The act of mercy is birthed in humility. As we saw in the passage for today, the Pharisee was confident he was doing all the right things. His heart was rooted in pride. But the publican knew he needed help. He knew he made mistakes and committed sin. Jesus made it clear to us through this parable that the one who asked for mercy out of a heart of humility received the mercy he needed. Jesus also emphasized that the Pharisee who had exalted himself would at some point be humbled. He would at some point find himself in a position where he realized he needed mercy. But by then, without a change of heart, it would be too late to access it.

Similarly, when you and I go through our lives with a heart of pride and a lack of willingness to address the sins that are creating the misery and chaos that consume us, we will neither show others mercy nor receive any for ourselves. Yet we can rest assured there will come a day when we will know how much we need it.

When you call out to God for mercy, keep in mind that your previous actions will affect how He responds to you. Do not blame God if He withholds mercy you feel like you need. You might want to assess your past history and whether or not you showed mercy to others in their times of need as well.

You can always request mercy, but you can never demand it. And while God is rich in mercy, He decides how much to give predicated on what you have done to others.

Reaction: Which of the two men in the parable do you most identify with and why?

Why do you think God responded favorably to the tax collector and not the Pharisee?

In what ways can you proactively look for ways to show mercy to others?

Prayer : *Jesus, forgive me, for I am a sinner. I humbly bow before You and ask that You will forgive any and all pride that rises in my heart causing me to believe I am better than anyone else You have created. I want to show mercy to others, and I want to receive Your mercy, but I first ask that You will bless me with a spirit of humility so I can do that. In Your name I pray, amen.*

Thirty-Eight

> For the LORD your God is a merciful God; he will not
> abandon or destroy you or forget the covenant with
> your ancestors, which he confirmed to them by oath.
>
> Deuteronomy 4:31 NIV

There are many reasons that people need mercy, but one of them is when circumstances outside of their control have caused chaos in their lives. It could be that a person was born blind or handicapped in some way. It could be that a weather catastrophe occurred in their region. It could be due to cutbacks at work, or an accident on the job or on the road. There are countless reasons why people are miserable due to no fault of their own. We've all experienced these times as well. It is during these seasons or situations, where we need someone to intervene and lift the burden of misery we cannot control, that we discover how refreshing mercy can truly be.

But it is also in these times, when the weight of the world looms heavy on our shoulders, that God also looks at our track record of whether or not we showed mercy to those in need. We will be blessed with God's mercy if we have been merciful to others.

Granted, this is contrary to the dog-eat-dog society we live in. But it is a kingdom value that, if you fail to apply it regularly to others, will come back to bite you as well.

Now, I understand, you can't help everyone. No one has the capacity to help everyone. But to live with this kingdom value of mercy means that you do make an effort to remove the burden and lessen the misery for those whom you can. You can make showing mercy a lifestyle and not an event.

It starts with altering your viewpoint to one that is rooted in humility. As you grow in this area, you will begin to judge less and help more. Mercy is a natural outgrowth of kingdom living. It is a natural outgrowth of having a right relationship with God in such a way that you understand and accept the mercy He has shown to you. Anytime you dismiss God's work of mercy in your own life, beginning with salvation, you will be less likely to show mercy to others.

Outward mercy is an indicator light for your inward level of humility and gentleness. You'll see that many of these kingdom virtues rest on each other. They are intertwined with each other. As you grow in spiritual maturity with regard to one, you will often grow in spiritual maturity with regard to others. That's why it is so important to spend focused and dedicated time with Jesus Christ. He is the supreme example of what it means to have a heart rooted in kingdom values. As you spend time with Jesus both through His Word and in prayer, you will become more like Him. He will begin to rub off on you. Then, people will know you are His disciple because you will exhibit the kingdom values He so longs for you to have.

Reaction: What is one thing from your past that emotionally hinders you from showing mercy to others?

What are you willing to do to overcome this hindrance?

Why do you think Jesus wants you to be able to show mercy more easily and effortlessly toward others?

Prayer: Jesus, the things that have taken place in my life that have hardened my heart can oftentimes be a hindrance to showing mercy toward others. I want to overcome these things so that I can serve You more completely. Help me identify these things and address them both emotionally and spiritually so that I can fully heal. I pray all of this in Your name, amen.

Thirty-Nine

> Remember me for this, O my God, and do not blot
> out my loyal deeds which I have performed for the
> house of my God and its services.
>
> Nehemiah 13:14

If you want God to relieve your burdens and lighten your load, you need to stop skipping over the opportunities He gives you to do the same for others around you. What goes around really does come around when it has to do with kingdom values.

Have you ever been on a customer service call and been told that this call is being recorded for quality assurance? The business managers do that so they can go back and double-check that their customer service agents are operating according to the standards they have established. Likewise, when you call on God for mercy, He has some kingdom values standards established, and He is going to double-check if you've been adhering to them. This may be a selfish way of looking at why you should show mercy, but this is how Jesus framed it. He made it clear that those who show mercy will be shown mercy. Or, if you want to reverse that—those who do not show mercy run the risk of not being shown mercy when they need it.

Of course, God can always go outside of His prescribed plans anytime He wants to do so. He can show mercy to whomever He wants to at any time He wants to. But what Jesus is stressing in this kingdom value is that there exists a boomerang effect when you show mercy. Or, another way to state it in today's contemporary language is that there exists an incentive to showing mercy. The more you give, the more you set yourself up to receive. What's more, you can feel confident in asking God to give it to you if you have a track record of showing mercy.

Nehemiah is a perfect example of this in the Bible. Throughout the book, we see Nehemiah doing good to those in need. He had a comfortable position in a comfortable location with a comfortable outlook on life. After all, he was the cupbearer to the king of Persia. But despite his comfort, Nehemiah's heart became burdened for his people, the Israelites. His heart became broken over the plight of Jerusalem.

So, in the book named after him in Scripture, we see Nehemiah leaving the comfort of his surroundings and going out to help people who are hurting. He leads the campaign to rebuild the walls of Jerusalem. He brings justice to a group of people who were being treated unjustly. He feeds and clothes people who need it, and he supplies and enables them to defend themselves, their families, and the city.

Yet as you read through the struggles and difficulties Nehemiah had to overcome in order to bring about such good for others, you see a repeated phrase. It's a short phrase, and you might have missed it if you read the chapters too quickly. But often throughout the book you will find the phrase, "remember me for good."

As Nehemiah is going about doing good for others and showing mercy to those in need, Nehemiah is looking up to God in heaven and nudging Him with this phrase, "remember me for good." In other words, He is asking God to take note. He's asking God to keep track. He's asking God to return the kindness to him when he needs it most. Nehemiah prays this way because Nehemiah knew the kingdom principle that giving sets you up to receive. That's what the Bible means when it says you are more blessed to give than to receive (Acts 20:35).

Reaction: Have you ever asked God to specifically remember the good and merciful things you have done for others when asking Him to show mercy to you? If yes, what was the result?

Why is it important to point out the things you have done for others when praying to God?

Have you been encouraged by helping someone else, and how did that impact your desire to help others even more?

Prayer: *Jesus, remember me for good when You think of my life and the things that I need regarding Your mercy, comfort, and care. Remember the times when no one else even noticed, but You did. Remember my loyalty to Your Word and my faithfulness to Your commands. In Your name I pray, amen.*

Forty

"Blessed are the pure in heart, for they shall see God."

Matthew 5:8

To see God who is holy means we need to look toward Him with spiritual eyes. We need to purify our hearts. We are told that we are blessed when we have pure hearts, and we will see God as a result. Many of us are not seeing God for ourselves because we are taking in that which has contaminated our spiritual systems. We are allowing in the pollutants of the culture, which then produce watery, itchy spiritual eyes. Anyone knows that it is more difficult to see clearly when your eyes are watering and red. These cultural contaminants cloud our vision to such a degree that we no longer recognize or experience His work, power, provision, transformation, deliverance, and victory firsthand. Sure, we may hear about these things from others, but when we look around our own lives, we cannot see God up close and personal for ourselves.

To see God, your heart must be pure. Your heart must be undefiled. Spiritually speaking, a pure heart means singleness of devotion. It means to love all of God with all of you, not just a portion of you for a time. Purity of heart means you are no longer disconnected from God by allowing something else to defile your relationship with Him.

As we've seen earlier through some of the other kingdom values, God and sin are irreconcilable. The two don't get along. You wouldn't want to live in a house with rotten garbage piled up all around you, and neither does God want to abide in the temples of our souls with rotten, sinful garbage. In order to get rid of the trash in our homes, we take it out. Similarly, we must repent of sin and turn from it in order to be clean within and have a pure heart. God simply can't be comfortable where unrighteousness is allowed to express itself freely.

This description of being "pure in heart" has to do with not allowing the contaminants of sin to penetrate the heart so as to cause God to have to remove himself or to distance himself from intimacy with you. Many Christians today carry on a long-distance relationship with God. They are more like Pluto than Mercury. They are a long way off. And because they are a long way off, they are cold like Pluto, too. The further you are from the proximity of God, the colder your heart grows because He is the Source of love, compassion, and light.

What Jesus reminds us in this kingdom value is that if we are going to get to see God at a more intimate level than the average person does, and if we are going to experience God more deeply than we ever have before, then we must chase after the cleansing of our hearts. We must live with a pursuit of purity.

Now, don't misunderstand this. Jesus' concern is about purity—real purity. It's easy to camouflage ourselves so that we look a lot cleaner than we are. We can dust off some wrong desires or scrub away some sin for a season. It's easy to mask unrighteousness with a righteous look or by saying seemingly righteous sayings. Jesus knows us intimately and can see through any façade we may erect to fool people around us. That's why He called the Pharisees out like He did when He said, "Woe to you, scribes and Pharisees, hypocrites! For you clean the outside of the cup and of the dish, but inside they are full of robbery and self-indulgence" (Matthew 23:25).

In other words, Jesus told them He saw through their external façade that made it appear they were on the up and up. He saw past their external attire that made it look like they and God were running buddies. He didn't fall for their fancy words or inside jokes that made it seem like they were hanging out with God on the regular. No, Jesus told them they were nothing but whitewashed tombs full of dead men's bones. A whitewashed tomb may appear crisp and clean on the outside, but once you peer inside, you'll find nothing but stench, rot, and filth of all kinds.

God is not after a purity of look, or a purity of location, or even a purity of religious activity. None of that matters if the heart itself is impure. None of that means anything if you have a heart far removed from God. In order to see God and recognize His hand in your life and His guidance to your heart, you must purify your heart so that you can dwell near Him, in close proximity relationally.

Reaction: What is one thing you can work on to help purify your heart more than it is right now?

What are some hesitations you may have toward purifying your heart, if any?

What happens in your life when you draw close to God and recognize His hand in your life?

Prayer: *Jesus, purify my heart to such a degree that enables me to clearly see God and His work in my life. I repent of the sin that contaminates my life. I want to be rid of bitterness, unforgiveness, and all other sins that I have become comfortable with allowing. Help me be pure, Jesus, as You are pure. I pray this in Your name, amen.*

Forty-One

"He who has My commandments and keeps them is the one who loves Me; and he who loves Me will be loved by My Father, and I will love him and will disclose Myself to him."

John 14:21

Many of us have water filter systems in our homes. We don't drink the tap water. Instead, we take the water and run it through a filtering system to remove the impurities or toxins within. This is because we do not want the invisible bacteria, chemicals, and additives to harm our bodies. We want to drink that which is pure, undefiled, and healthy. In fact, many of us have gone so far as to put whole-house water filter systems in place, at no small expense. Or we place water filters on our showers as well. Pure water is a source of life to our bodies, while contaminated water is a source of disease and ailments.

How we feel about our water, God feels about our hearts. He knows that the contaminants of sin and the pollutants of pride only harm a person's life. He doesn't want to see our hearts impure, not only because it offends Him, but also because He knows how it destroys us. It destroys our relationships and thought processes, and even damages our dreams and destinies. Just as impurities cloud the water so you can no longer see the pristine nature of what it is, impurities also cloud our hearts, bubbling over to impact our spiritual vision as well. We can no longer see the pristine nature of who God is and what He has placed within us.

Seeing God is important in life because it helps us see everything around us through a spiritual lens. God is Spirit. To know Him intimately is to know His heart. It is to know His perspective. It is to see life from His viewpoint. It is to live with a kingdom perspective. When you can view your life through the lens of the Holy Spirit, you don't see people and problems like you used to. You see more than the limited physical realm in front of you.

But when you are not connected to God, you will not be able to see Him and see through His spiritual eyes. A lot of the misery we experience in life is due to being a slave to what we see. We assume that what we see is all there is to reality because we cannot see from God's perspective. God can see so much more than we can. He can see what is behind, in front of, and all around. He is not bound by the physical limitations that we are. He can see all aspects of all things.

When you live according to the kingdom value of a pure spiritual heart, you will grow to see more through God's eyes. You gain an entrance into His eternal perspective. Seeing God means perceiving and sensing His reality. It opens up windows all around us through which we can gain clarity. Like the servant who was limited by physical eyesight when he looked out over the territory and only saw the approaching army, seeing God enables us to be like Elisha, who prayed that God would open his servant's eyes. The servant was alarmed at the strength of the army circling the city. But when God opened his spiritual eyes, the servant saw God's warrior angels lined up to protect and defend them (2 Kings 6:15–18).

How many battles have you gone out to fight that God had already planned to defend you from to begin with? How many battle scars have you needlessly obtained attempting to wage spiritual warfare with physical weapons? Seeing God because you live with this kingdom value of pureness of heart gives you the ability to see life spiritually. You can see His hand steering you away from danger in time. You can see His heart lovingly directing you toward your destiny. You can see the potential pitfalls on the path you've chosen so that you can avoid them rather than fall into them. Seeing God means you will see what you need in order to live your life to the fullest. It is something we all need.

Reaction: What is your perspective of God?

What ways can you help yourself see Him more fully?

What would you like to have improved in your life through a closer relationship with God?

Prayer: *Jesus, help me to see my life and everything that takes place around me through spiritual eyes. Show me what is truly happening and not just what I can see on the surface. Give me eyes to see You, and in doing so, I will see spiritually. In Your name I pray, amen.*

Forty-Two

> But he must ask in faith without any doubting, for the one who doubts is like the surf of the sea, driven and tossed by the wind. For that man ought not to expect that he will receive anything from the Lord, being a double-minded man, unstable in all his ways.
>
> James 1:6–8

When you see God, He shows you what He is up to. He shows you what He is doing. He pulls back the curtain and reveals the activity and purposes behind the veil. When you see God, He can even reveal to you why things happened to you in your past in order to get you to your present. He can show you what you need to do now in order to make a better tomorrow.

Seeing God isn't the same as staring at a piece of art on a wall. He is not just something to admire and praise. Seeing God allows you to see yourself. It allows you to see that you are a reflection of Him made in His image. It enables you to see why you were created and what you have been brought here to do. Seeing God peels off the cataracts clouding your spiritual eyes and reveals the working and mysteries of the spiritual realm. With this insight, you can then navigate your days and your nights with wisdom.

The psalmist reminds us that purity of heart enables God to hear us when we pray (Psalm 66:18). It opens the floodgates of His goodness (Psalm 73:1). The writer of Hebrews puts it like this: "Pursue peace with all men, and the sanctification without which no one will see the Lord" (Hebrews 12:14). The real experience of God working, operating, moving, leading, governing, guiding, and blessing your life flows out of the abundance of a pure heart. It flows from the springs of a sanctified soul.

Life is too complicated and lies are too frequent to rely on your physical understanding, especially these days. It's hard to tell who is telling the truth anymore when you turn on the news, or go on social media, or listen to your friends or family. It's like the world has turned into one continuous round of the old telephone game where misinterpretation after misinterpretation is all we have left to go on.

In the chaos of our culture today, you do not want to live limited to what you can merely see physically. You do not want to have to depend on your five senses only. Only God offers a way to see things from His unlimited vantage point. But to do so means that you must be pure of heart. You don't get to access this blessing when you have a soul contaminated with sin. One of the primary sources of sin entering our lives comes through our minds. If you can get your mind right, the rest will follow. James states it like this:

> You lust and do not have; so you commit murder. You are envious and cannot obtain; so you fight and quarrel. You do not have because you do not ask. You ask and do not receive, because you ask with wrong motives, so that you may spend it on your pleasures. You adulteresses, do you not know that friendship with the world is hostility toward God?
>
> Therefore whoever wishes to be a friend of the world makes himself an enemy of God. Or do you think that the Scripture speaks to no purpose: "He jealously desires the Spirit which He has made to dwell in us"? But He gives a greater grace. Therefore it says, "God is opposed to the proud, but gives grace to the humble." Submit therefore to God. Resist the devil and he will flee from you.
>
> Draw near to God and He will draw near to you. Cleanse your hands, you sinners; and purify your hearts, you double-minded.
>
> James 4:2–8

The way to purify your heart is to get rid of your double-mindedness. Double means two. Double-mindedness means you are thinking two different ways at the same time. You are carrying the Bible in one hand and the world in another. In order for you to resist the devil, you need to position yourself so that God is not resisting you. It is through your attachment to God and His kingdom authority manifest in the blood of Jesus Christ that you will gain access to the upper hand. But you can only attach yourself to God in this way when you approach Him with purity of heart.

Reaction: Describe double-mindedness in your own words.

Is it possible for a person to be unaware of being double-minded, and if so, what would be the result?

In what ways have you seen God clarify your thoughts spiritually?

Prayer: *Jesus, free me from the bondage of living with a double mind. I want to solely focus on You and live for You in all things. You are my hope and my help, and I worship You always. I pray this in Your name, amen.*

Forty-Three

"Blessed are the peacemakers, for they shall be called sons of God."

Matthew 5:9

Whatever the case and wherever it may appear, it looks like everywhere you turn these days there is a war. The same was a common occurrence in Jesus' day as well. That's why the kingdom value that focuses on peace is so important. We read, "Blessed are the peacemakers, for they shall be called sons of God" (Matthew 5:9).

Peace is harmony where conflict used to exist. Peace is more than a truce. After all, two people or two nations can stop fighting physically but still live in a cold war. Some married couples assume they have peace in their relationship because they don't talk to each other. But that is not peace. That's a relational cold war. We should never be satisfied with a cold war and think it means we have peace. Peace is much more than the removal of overt conflict. Peace includes resolving the conflict by exposing the source of the contention in order to address it.

To live with this kingdom value of peacemaking is to live as someone who does not run away from conflict, but rather faces the conflict with truth in such a way so as to resolve it. A peacemaker is more than a peacekeeper. It's more than someone who stands between those in conflict and tells them not to fight. A peacemaker looks for a way to resolve the conflict at hand. A peacemaker ought to be able to step back from the combatants and have them continue to get along because they have experienced a real resolution to the problem.

This is why peace must always be accompanied by righteousness. Psalm 85:10 explains this relationship: "Lovingkindness and truth have met together; righteousness and peace have kissed each other." When love and truth meet, the mouths of righteousness and peace similarly connect, producing the necessary results.

Hebrews 12:14 describes the connection like this: "Pursue peace with all men, and the sanctification without which no one will see the Lord." We are to pursue peace, but we must remember that this pursuit cannot be absent of sanctification. That is, we could pursue peace, but we cannot obtain it without the righteous requirements of God.

When Adam and Eve sinned against God, they created conflict. They created conflict with God, conflict with each other, and conflict within their own nature. This conflict resulted from their sin. It wasn't until the sin was addressed that the conflict could be addressed.

Peace is a bridge between truth and righteousness. Both truth and righteousness must exist if there is going to be any amount of lasting peace.

When a woman wants to straighten the curls in her hair, the beautician will add a chemical treatment to neutralize the impact of a perm. The purpose of the neutralizing agent is to keep the perm from doing chemical damage to the hair. In other words, if the perm is left in the hair and not neutralized, it will wind up doing more damage than good. Similarly, a peace-maker is someone who enters a scene of conflict in order to neutralize the conflict so that further damage is not allowed to occur.

To be a peacemaker is to be someone who is actively involved in creating harmony where conflict once existed. For those who choose to intentionally live according to this kingdom value, the blessing you will receive is that you will be "called sons of God."

Reaction: Describe the difference between being a peacemaker and a peacekeeper.

In what ways do you actively pursue peacemaking in your life?

What do you think are some of the reasons Satan seeks to disrupt the peace in our world and in believers' lives?

Prayer : *Jesus, give me greater discernment to be able to identify when Satan is disrupting the peace. Help me be aware so that I do not fall into the trap of division and sowing discord among those in my sphere of influence. In Your name I pray, amen.*

Forty-Four

For a child will be born to us, a son will be given to us;
And the government will rest on His shoulders;
And His name will be called Wonderful Counselor,
Mighty God,
Eternal Father, Prince of Peace.

Isaiah 9:6

To live as a peacemaker is to live as someone who truly reflects God. As a result, you will then be called, or known as, the son or daughter of God because you reflect His character.

The Bible tells us that God's character is composed of peace. We read that God is a God of peace (1 Corinthians 14:33). Jesus is known as the "Prince of Peace" (Isaiah 9:6). His birth ushers in a season of "peace among men with whom He is pleased" (Luke 2:14). Jesus told His disciples that His attribute of peace is what He would leave with them (John 14:27). In fact, when you read through the New Testament, you'll see that many of the epistles are introduced by the words "Grace to you and peace."

Peace is a central component of the character of Christ. That's why to live as a peacemaker is to publicly identify with God. It is to publicly align yourself underneath this key kingdom value. When you do that, you will be blessed by being recognized as God's son or God's daughter.

To be called the son or daughter of God is to be referred to as someone who knows God intimately. This is because if you share the character of God where His character has rubbed off on your own, that means you have close contact with God. I'm sure you've seen a married couple who, over time, start to look like each other. And I'm sure you've heard a married couple talk and finish each other's sentences. This is because, over time, they begin to rub off on each other. Their mannerisms, styles, and even their expressions become more closely aligned as they spend a greater amount of time together.

To be so close with God that you reflect His mannerisms, heart, and even His expressions reveals this intimacy to a watching world. When you live with this kingdom value, or even with all the kingdom values we are exploring in our time together, you are reflecting your intimacy with the King. Conversely, if you are living with an attitude and character of conflict, bitterness, and divisiveness, you are reflecting the closeness you share with the devil.

Satan's agenda is to create conflict. His agenda is to divide. The reason he makes this his overarching goal is because he knows that God is a God of unity. He knows that God is a God of peace. Anytime Satan can get believers quarreling or divisive, he is taking aim at the very heart of God. Satan knows that God does not hang out with division. God does not abide in disunity.

Conflict within families is one of the devil's favorite forms of disunity. He enjoys stirring things up between parents and children as well as between siblings, and especially between husbands and wives. Satan knows that if a husband isn't living in a considerate manner with his wife, his prayers will be hindered (see 1 Peter 3:7). A favorite pastime of Satan's is sowing bitterness, arguing, and confusion in the church. The more he can divide us, the more power has over us because he has distanced us from the only thing able to overpower him: the kingdom authority of God. In addition to spreading dissent among believers, Satan is working overtime to divide people in all sorts of ways in the culture at large.

Satan is not solely after you in destroying your emotions or disturbing your thoughts. In doing so, he's after everyone else as well. The more people with messed up emotions and destructive thoughts living together or interacting together or working together, the easier it is to keep people apart. And when Satan keeps people apart, he also successfully keeps them from being able to access the authority of heaven in a hellish world.

When you and I resort to living as conflict contributors rather than as peacemakers, we have inadvertently chosen sides. We have aligned ourselves with the agenda of the devil. God is a God of harmony and oneness. That doesn't mean we all have to agree or see things the same way, but it does mean that in our disagreements, we express ourselves in a way that demonstrates we are unified on a common goal—that of advancing God's kingdom agenda on earth.

Reaction: Describe the link between seeking peace and experiencing peace.

Why do you think Satan likes to go after your thoughts when trying to disrupt your peace?

What practice can you put in place to help you protect and preserve the level of peace you experience in your personal life?

Prayer: *Jesus, I want to master my emotions and thoughts to such a degree that I do not give in to Satan's ploys and strategies as he seeks to trip me up. Help me recognize his tactics so that I do not go down a path of disunity in any area of my life. I love You and want to reflect You in all I do. In Your name I pray, amen.*

Forty-Five

If possible, so far as it depends on you, be at peace
with all men.

Romans 12:18

Peace is good for us personally, but it is also critical for
us relationally with God. Our peace with others opens
up the flow of God's relational presence and work in
our lives. Far too many of us are actually blocking the
movement of God in our lives because we are living
in ongoing conflict. Or we are blocking the authority
of God to overpower the enemy and his tactics in our
lives because we are engaged in disunity.

When our emotions and our thoughts are war zones
due to a refusal to be unified under God and His kingdom authority, we pay the price. You may think that
when you are angry at someone or judging someone
you disagree with that you are harming or dismiss-
ing them. But you are actually harming and dismiss-
ing yourself. The more conflict you carry in your own
heart, the more chaos you invite into your life and
circumstances.

Blessed are the peacemakers because they will carry
the powerful testimony of the power of God. To be
blessed is to have God show up when you need Him

most. It is to see God's hand in the midst of your trials and challenges. It is to experience the authority of God as He overturns, overrides, or removes that which Satan has sent to take you down. A blessing isn't a pat on your head or an "atta boy" on your back. A blessing accesses power, opportunities, and kingdom authority. A blessing opens doors.

This concept of living according to the kingdom value of being a peacemaker isn't just for monks or nuns or people picketing for peace. This is a critical kingdom value which, if you adopt it as a way of life, will open the floodgates of heaven for you. This divine recognition of your position as a son or daughter of God gives you instant access to the King. It gives you access to answered prayer. You get to hear from heaven, whereas before your prayers often bounced off the ceiling. Answered prayer is a two-way commitment. Prayer isn't about just sending up a wish list to God and He acts as your dutiful servant to fulfill it. Answered prayer is frequently predicated on your relationship to God and your obedience to His commands.

If you want to see and experience more of God in your life, then you need to make the pursuit of peace a high commitment in your heart. It is in how you treat others that you reflect the level of God's love that is radiating inside you. When you cannot see what to do at all, allow God to do wonders by simply pursuing peace with those around you.

Reaction: How can the pursuit of peace in your relationships allow you to experience God more freely?

According to God's Word, is there ever a time to accept disunity? If so, when?

What areas or relationships in your life could benefit by your prioritization of the pursuit of peace?

Prayer: *Jesus, give me inner peace so that it radiates from within me to those around me. I welcome more of You and Your presence within me so that Your love and peace overflow from me to others. I pray this in Your name, amen.*

Forty-Six

> "Blessed are you when people insult you and persecute you, and falsely say all kinds of evil against you because of Me. Rejoice and be glad, for your reward in heaven is great; for in the same way they persecuted the prophets who were before you."
>
> Matthew 5:11–12

The last kingdom value given to us in the Sermon on the Mount isn't one that we often post on social media. It's not one we frame and hang on our wall, either. It's a hard one to wrap our minds around sometimes, especially in a culture and world that promote personal happiness in the present moment. This kingdom value might even make most of us nervous just by reading it. Jesus didn't mince His words when He gave it to us, either. So the best way to approach it is to embrace it. The final kingdom value we are to live out is told to us like this: "Blessed are those who have been persecuted for the sake of righteousness, for theirs is the kingdom of heaven" (Matthew 5:10).

Now, if that didn't scare you off enough to close this devotional—or to turn and walk away if you were one of those gathered by the Sea of Galilee that day— Jesus takes a moment to emphasize this again in the following two verses, which are listed as our daily Scripture reading. All the other kingdom values are delivered in one succinct sentence. But this one gets a double punch. Jesus continues, just in case anyone missed what He said. He wanted us to truly grasp this.

But notice that this double-punch kingdom value also comes with a double blessing. Every other value gives you one blessing, but this one doubles the fun. Jesus reminds His listeners that you are doubly blessed when you are persecuted, insulted, and maligned for the sake of righteousness and His kingdom.

But even though He says it clearly and says it twice, it still seems to be incongruent because we don't normally associate a blessing with hardship and persecution. We don't naturally connect these things. When we dig deeper into the meaning of the term used here for *persecution* in the Greek language, it makes it even more difficult to see the connection. The literal translation means "to be harassed." It refers to being treated in an evil, negative manner. This can include insults, abuse, vicious speech, and even false accusations.

Just writing those things down makes me wince. It probably does the same for you when you read them. None of us enjoys being bullied. None of us volunteers for harassment. But Jesus concludes His emphasis on kingdom values by saying we are blessed for being bullied for righteousness' sake. Keep in mind, He doesn't say you and I are blessed for being bullied for any reason. The blessing is tied to the "why" behind it.

This blessing is given to those who are persecuted or harassed for the sake of His name, His righteousness, or His kingdom agenda. This type of persecution comes about when you are choosing to do or say the right thing for righteous reasons, and you face a fallout for your choice. Facing persecution because you are living out the values of the kingdom of God and you are associated with Jesus Christ is when you can expect a blessing.

Reaction: Why is it important to understand this kingdom value even though it may make us feel uncomfortable?

What does being "persecuted for righteousness" mean to you personally?

What is one way to overcome any hesitation you may have toward living out this kingdom value?

Prayer: Jesus, enable me to see the big picture when things don't go well. Show me how to look for the blessing when I'm facing various trials related to living for Your kingdom. I want to praise You even in the midst of the difficult seasons of life. In Your name I pray, amen.

Forty-Seven

> "Remember the word that I said to you, 'A slave is not greater than his master.' If they persecuted Me, they will also persecute you; if they kept My word, they will keep yours also. But all these things they will do to you for My name's sake, because they do not know the One who sent Me."

John 15:20–21

If you are not facing spiritual persecution or opposition of any kind, then you can pretty much assume that you are not living a godly life based on kingdom values. If there are absolutely no negative repercussions coming upon you because of your faith and the choices you make based on your faith, then your faith is not being clearly demonstrated. You are a secret-agent Christian, or a spiritual CIA representative. Persecution is part and parcel to the process of kingdom living.

When you decided to live as a visible Christian because you wanted to align yourself with the values system of the kingdom of God, you decided to be a problem within this postmodern age. In this postmodern period, Christian values are no longer the normative values system of the culture. The further a culture moves away from a Christian worldview, the more those who hold to and live according to kingdom values will appear to be peculiar and will be persecuted.

Now, to appear peculiar doesn't mean you are to intentionally be weird. It just means you will stand out as stepping to the beat of a different drum. You will set yourself apart from the crowd as someone who listens to a different voice and adheres to a different standard called righteousness. Jesus' standard of kingdom values is diametrically opposed to the world's values. When you choose to embrace His kingdom standard as a lifestyle, you will invite spiritual persecution or harassment into your world.

I am sure that you had someone in your class in school, like I did, who would "set the curve." When the teacher said he or she would grade on the curve, that meant the highest score would serve as the perfect score. In that case, most of us hoped that the highest score wouldn't be that high at all. But there was always somebody who would ace the test, it seems. There was always someone who had to ruin the blessing of the curve for the rest of us.

See, the problem with Jesus is that whenever He—or His kingdom values—shows up, He messes with the world's curve. He sets the standard too high. He raises the bar. As long as people can compare themselves with other people, everyone passes. But when Jesus and His kingdom values appear, problems pop up for everyone else. Jesus reveals the righteous standards of God.

And when you and I choose to live according to these righteous standards, we make other people—and their lower standards—look bad. We demonstrate that peace is more productive than chaos. We demonstrate that love is more powerful than hate. We reveal that families can stay together and employees can work hard, even when no one is around to see what they are doing. We raise the standard, and in doing so, we invite persecution.

Nobody likes someone else to show up and reveal just how far they are lagging. Jesus did that when He came to earth. And we do that as His kingdom disciples when we live out the kingdom values He's established for us. So, just as Jesus was persecuted when He walked down here, we can expect the same. In fact, He tells us that in the book of John, which we read as our Scripture passage for today.

You can see in that passage that what they did to Jesus, they will do to you if and when you choose to follow Jesus as your Lord and King. As you adopt more and more of the kingdom values into your life, you will be manifesting the presence of Christ to others. The same level of hate, vitriol, and persecution that He experienced has the potential to come at you as well.

Unfortunately, the reason so many of us do not face any spiritual persecution is because we are not living with kingdom values. But with spiritual persecution comes the promise of blessing. So in order to pursue these special spiritual blessings, we need to be open to the working of God in and through our lives through this particular kingdom value.

Reaction: Which of the kingdom values that we have looked at so far is the easiest for you to live out and why?

Which of the kingdom values that we have looked at so far is the most challenging to live out and why?

What can you learn from the easiest kingdom value to live out that can help you with the challenging one?

Prayer: *Jesus, I want to be a well-rounded kingdom disciple living out all the kingdom values You have called me to. Help me not to neglect the ones that are more difficult, as I want to show the world a reflection of You in me. I pray this in Your name, amen.*

Forty-Eight

> "But seek first His kingdom and His righteousness,
> and all these things will be added to you."
>
> Matthew 6:33

In the past, we often saw great hatred toward our nation due to our association with Israel. Since Israel was hated deeply by many nations, our public association with Israel brought animosity toward us as well. What Jesus is saying in this final kingdom value is that if and when you publicly align with Him and claim His kingdom values system as your own, others are going to feel about you what they feel about Him. And since they obviously didn't want Him—they even crucified Him—you can expect the same level of disdain toward you.

The issue you'll face when you adopt a kingdom values system is that Christ's values system conflicts with the system of this world order. There's a clash of opinions that will show up in how you wind up being treated. As you adopt the values of the kingdom, it will create issues. It will provoke insults. It could negatively impact your potential for promotion or a raise at work. It could negatively impact who likes you on the job. It could negatively impact who invites you to lunch during break. Living and speaking according to the ethics of the kingdom will affect your associations elsewhere. This is because living with a kingdom values system in the midst of a world that doesn't buy into that values system will invite rejection and hate.

Last I checked, none of us want to experience rejection. None of us enjoy experiencing hate. And it's natural not to want these things in your life. So, in order to truly live according to the kingdom values system, you're going to need to resist the urge to tweak it to fit the culture. You're going to need to resist your internal impulse to stay under the radar of those around you. You're going to need to dig deep and discover the courage and bravery that is required for standing up in defense of the truth, which is so frequently attacked and maligned today.

You can't change the kingdom values and still access the blessing. You can't rewrite them and expect to get the favor from God that is tied to them. His blessing comes when you adopt His values and live them out in your life.

What God desires in establishing this incentivized kingdom values system is maintaining a standard of righteousness in an evil-infiltrated world. He has not changed His standard just because society ignores it. He desires that we rise up to it as a way of manifesting Him and His presence to those around us. When we do that, we call attention to Him. We bring Him glory. We honor Him as we point out just how far off the mark Satan's world order truly is, as well as those who have chosen to operate by it.

When you and I carry the light of the values of the kingdom within the spheres of influence we live in, we reflect God's standard to others. We help others to see where they need to adjust, repent, and grow as well. Sure, they may not like that. They may not appreciate that. But if they respond to God's kingdom standard themselves, they will eventually be blessed by it, too.

Reaction: Why is it important to replace your standards with God's?

What is one specific standard you need to align more with God's?

Describe the challenges you have to raising this standard in your own life.

Prayer: Jesus, help me to live according to Your righteous standards and seek Your kingdom above all else. Show me how to glorify You in everything that I do because I want to honor You always. In Your name I pray, amen.

Forty-Nine

He who walks righteously and speaks with sincerity,
He who rejects unjust gain
And shakes his hands so that they hold no bribe;
He who stops his ears from hearing about bloodshed
And shuts his eyes from looking upon evil;
He will dwell on the heights,
His refuge will be the impregnable rock;
His bread will be given him,
His water will be sure.

Your eyes will see the King in His beauty;
They will behold a far-distant land.

Isaiah 33:15–17

Applying kingdom values to your thoughts, words, and actions should be a regular pursuit. If it falls to the wayside due to the busy schedules and distractions in life, then the close relationship you desire with God will also grow more distant. This is because God has given us these kingdom values as a way of reflecting Him to a world in need. He desires to be close to those of us who have hearts that honor Him through aligning ourselves underneath Him.

It may become easy to neglect pursuing the kingdom values in your life, though, because it brings many bumps and potential bruises with it. But remember that the people who experience negative repercussions due to their identification with Christ and His kingdom values system will also get to see heaven overrule earth. There is a benefit to the pain. Instead of being entwined and trapped in the kingdom of earth, where men or the devil and his minions rule, you will get to see the kingdom of heaven where God rules.

When it appears that the earth's kingdom is keeping you from moving ahead, either through denying you a promotion or excluding you from activities, you will get to see what happens when God demonstrates that He is the ultimate ruler over all. Society may seek to control your mind, emotions, or even your productivity—but society will have to yield to God when you invite Him in to intervene. If you hold to His kingdom values system, He will override the systems of this age.

As a kingdom follower, you will know what it means for the supernatural to invade the natural. You will know firsthand what it looks like for heaven to invade history. You'll get to experience eternity overruling earth. You'll get to see what God looks like when He shows up and shows out on your behalf.

One of the reasons so many of us have never seen God overrule anything, or anyone, in our lives is because we've not chosen to live according to kingdom values. We've never had a situation where God saw that we were acting and speaking according to His kingdom values so that He could act and speak in defense of us. God doesn't intervene just because we need it. He intervenes when He sees that we have chosen to live according to His established standard.

If you choose not to identify with the person or values of the King, you don't get to see the kingdom of heaven overruling the kingdom of men. This is a choice you get to make. Only you can make your choice for yourself. God will never force you to live your life as a committed kingdom disciple expressing His kingdom values to the world. That's one reason why He has made it so clear what the benefits are when we do live according to His Word. These benefits are meant to incentivize us toward a higher calling. Some of the benefits we will receive on earth. Other benefits won't come until eternity. But you can know for certain that God will reward a heart that seeks after Him and someone who models their life after His expressed kingdom values.

Reaction: What is one way you can be obedient to what God has revealed to you at this time?

Have you witnessed God show up for you when you had no way to show up for yourself, and what did you learn from that?

Why is it easy to want to give up when difficulties and trials come as a result of doing good?

Prayer: *Jesus, I don't want to waste my life living for myself. I want to honor You in all I do and say. Show me how I can do that more than I do right now. Help my heart to be rightly aligned underneath You as Lord and Savior of my soul. In Your name I pray, amen.*

Fifty

"Have I not commanded you? Be strong and coura-
geous! Do not tremble or be dismayed, for the Lord
your God is with you wherever you go."

Joshua 1:9

Getting to see heaven overrule earth when you play
by God's rules and keep His kingdom values first and
foremost in your life is one of life's greatest blessings.
Sure, the blessing is preceded by insults and possibly
even rejection. But when you get to see God show up in
a way you never could have imagined—a way you only
heard about on Sunday morning but never experienced
for yourself—that's when God becomes real. That's
when He starts to take shape in your life in such a way
that you can say you truly know Him.

We are to rejoice and be glad in the face of spiritually based harassment, similar to how disciples in the
book of Acts said they rejoiced in the midst of suffering
for their identification with Jesus Christ (see Acts 5:41).
The reason we rejoice is because it ultimately means
that heaven just got on our side.

Far too many of us live miserable lives because earth
is on our side, not heaven. Eternity and the authority
tied to it is not obligated to enter history and act on

your behalf if you refuse to live with kingdom values. God gets involved when He sees that you and I are honoring His goal of advancing His kingdom agenda on earth.

A lot of people want to presume that they are blessed and highly favored. They want to speak as if they have the Lord fighting their battles for them. But breathing is not a guarantee of God's divine intervention. Being alive on earth does not bind Him to your side. The way you get God's rule to overrule the chaos of the culture and the confusion in your circumstances is by aligning yourself under His rule. You do that by living out the kingdom values based on His truth that we have looked at in this book.

It starts with recognizing your own spiritual inadequacy. You begin by being poor in spirit. Then, you add to that a willingness to be honest about your sin and to mourn its existence in your life or in our land. Doing so enables you to then apply the kingdom value of gentleness to your words and your actions.

In addition to gentleness, and as you begin to see God's blessings flow more and more into your life, you develop a greater hunger and thirst for His righteousness. You pursue Him and His truth at a higher level because you want to apply His thoughts, His perspective, and His rule to your life. As you do, you'll discover that you have a greater level of mercy to show others. You will also start to live with a purity of heart that allows you to see God and His ways even more clearly than before. This will inspire you to be a peacemaker rather than a troublemaker in all you do and say.

And, as you will discover, living according to those kingdom values will usher upon you a level of persecution—insult, rejection, or even harassment—like you've never known before. But, as you'll see, even though it may be hard during the process, God will have your back in the long run. He will show up when you least expect it. And He will turn things around in your favor. Adopting a lifestyle of kingdom values will propel you into a future full of spiritual power, peace, and promise.

Reaction: Describe some of the most important spiritual truths you gained from this devotional.

In what ways have you experienced any life change during the time you've spent studying this topic?

Now that you have finished the devotional, what is your action plan to ensure that you do not lose any of the practical spiritual guidance you've gained?

Prayer: Jesus, give me greater courage to live out these kingdom values for You. Help me stay consistent in my pursuit of righteousness and the advancement of Your kingdom agenda on earth. I love You and praise You for bringing me this far. In Your name I pray, amen.

APPENDIX:
THE URBAN ALTERNATIVE

The Urban Alternative (TUA) equips, empowers, and unites Christians to impact *individuals, families, churches,* and *communities* through a thoroughly kingdom agenda worldview. In teaching truth, we seek to transform lives.

The core cause of the problems we face in our personal lives, homes, churches, and societies is a spiritual one; therefore, the only way to address it is spiritually. We've tried a political, social, economic, and even a religious agenda.

It's time for a **kingdom agenda**.

*The kingdom agenda can be defined as
the visible manifestation of the comprehensive
rule of God over every area of life.*

The unifying central theme throughout the Bible is the glory of God and the advancement of His kingdom.

The conjoining thread from Genesis to Revelation—from beginning to end—is focused on one thing: God's glory through advancing God's kingdom.

When you do not recognize that theme, the Bible becomes disconnected stories that are great for inspiration but seem to be unrelated in purpose and direction. Understanding the role of the kingdom in Scripture increases the relevancy of this several thousand-year-old text to your day-to-day living, because the kingdom is not only then; it is now.

The absence of the kingdom's influence in our personal lives, family lives, churches, and communities has led to a deterioration in our world of immense proportions:

- People live segmented, compartmentalized lives because they lack God's kingdom worldview.
- Families disintegrate because they exist for their own satisfaction rather than for the kingdom.
- Churches are limited in the scope of their impact because they fail to comprehend that the goal of the church is not the church itself, but the kingdom.
- Communities have nowhere to turn to find real solutions for real people who have real problems

because the church has become divided, in-grown, and unable to transform the cultural and political landscape in any relevant way.

The kingdom agenda offers us a way to see and live life with a solid hope by optimizing the solutions of heaven. When God is no longer the final and authoritative standard under which all else falls, order and hope leave with Him. But the reverse of that is true as well: as long as you have God, you have hope. If God is still in the picture, and as long as His agenda is still on the table, it's not over.

Even if relationships collapse, God will sustain you. Even if finances dwindle, God will keep you. Even if dreams die, God will revive you. As long as God and His rule are still the overarching standard in your life, family, church, and community, there is always hope.

Our world needs the King's agenda. Our churches need the King's agenda. Our families need the King's agenda.

We've put together a three-part plan to direct us to heal the divisions and strive for unity as we move toward the goal of truly being one nation under God. This three-part plan calls us to assemble with others in unity, address the issues that divide us, and to act together for social impact. Following this plan, we will see individuals, families, churches, and communities transformed as we follow God's kingdom agenda in every area of our lives. You can request this plan by emailing info@ tonyevans.org or by going online to tonyevans.org.

In many major cities, there is a loop that drivers can take when they want to get somewhere on the other side of the city but don't necessarily want to head straight through downtown. This loop will take you close enough to the city so that you can see its towering buildings and skyline, but not close enough to actually experience it.

This is precisely what we, as a culture, have done with God. We have put Him on the "loop" of our personal, family, church, and community lives. He's close enough to be at hand should we need Him in an emergency, but far enough away that He can't be the center of who we are.

We tend to want God on the "loop," not the King of the Bible who comes downtown into the very heart of our ways. Leaving God on the "loop" brings about dire consequences as we have seen in our own lives and with others. But when we make God, and His rule, the centerpiece of all we think, do, or say, it is then that we will experience Him in the way He longs for us to experience Him.

He wants us to be kingdom people with kingdom minds set on fulfilling His kingdom's purposes. He wants us to pray, as Jesus did, "Not my will, but Thy will be done." Because His is the kingdom, the power, and the glory.

There is only one God, and we are not Him. As King and Creator, God calls the shots. It is only when we align ourselves underneath His comprehensive hand that we will access His full power and authority in all spheres of life: personal, familial, ecclesiastical, and government.

As we learn how to govern ourselves under God, we then transform the institutions of family, church, and society using a biblically based kingdom worldview.

Under Him, we touch heaven and change earth.

To achieve our goal, we use a variety of strategies, approaches, and resources for reaching and equipping as many people as possible.

Broadcast Media

Millions of individuals experience *The Alternative with Dr. Tony Evans* through the daily radio broadcast playing on nearly **1,400 radio outlets** and in over **130 countries**. The broadcast can also be seen on several television networks and is available online at tonyevans .org. You can also listen or view the daily broadcast by downloading the Tony Evans app for free in the App store. Over 30 million message downloads/streams occur each year.

Leadership Training

The Tony Evans Training Center (TETC) facilitates a comprehensive discipleship platform, which provides an educational program that embodies the ministry philosophy of Dr. Tony Evans as expressed through the kingdom agenda. The training courses focus on leadership development and discipleship in the following five tracks:

- Bible and theology
- Personal growth
- Family and relationships
- Church health and leadership development
- Society and community impact strategies

The TETC program includes courses for both local and online students. Furthermore, TETC programming includes course work for non-student attendees. Pastors, Christian leaders, and Christian laity, both local and at a distance, can seek out The Kingdom Agenda Certificate for personal, spiritual, and professional development. For more information, visit: TonyEvansTraining.org

The Kingdom Agenda Pastors (KAP) provides a viable network for *like-minded pastors* who embrace the kingdom agenda philosophy. Pastors have the opportunity to go deeper with Dr. Tony Evans as they are given greater biblical knowledge, practical applications, and resources to impact individuals, families, churches, and communities. KAP welcomes *senior and associate pastors* of all churches. KAP also offers an annual Summit held each year in Dallas with intensive seminars, workshops, and resources. For more information, visit: KAFellowship.org

Pastors' Wives Ministry, founded by the late Dr. Lois Evans, provides *counsel*, *encouragement*, and *spiritual resources* for pastors' wives as they serve with their husbands in the ministry. A primary focus of the ministry is the KAP Summit that offers senior pastors' wives a safe place to *reflect*, *renew*, and *relax*, along with training in personal development, spiritual growth, and care for their emotional and physical well-being. For more information, visit: LoisEvans.org

Kingdom Community Impact

The outreach programs of The Urban Alternative seek to provide positive impact to individuals, churches, families, and communities through a variety of ministries. We see these efforts as necessary to our calling as a ministry and essential to the communities we serve. With training on how to initiate and maintain programs to adopt schools, or provide homeless services, or partner toward unity and justice with the local police precincts, which creates a connection between the police and our community, we, as a ministry, live out God's kingdom agenda according to our *Kingdom Strategy for Community Transformation*.

The Kingdom Strategy for Community Transformation is a three-part plan that equips churches to have a positive impact on their communities for the kingdom of God. It also provides numerous practical suggestions for how this three-part plan can be implemented in your community, and it serves as a blueprint for unifying churches around the common goal of creating a better world for all of us. For more information, visit: TonyEvans.org and click on the link to access the 3-Point Plan. A course for this strategy is also offered online through the Tony Evans Training Center.

Tony Evans Films ushers in positive life change through compelling video-shorts, animation, and feature-length films. We seek to build kingdom disciples through the power of story. We use a variety of platforms for viewer consumption and have over 120 million digital views. We also merge video-shorts and film with relevant Bible study materials to bring people to the saving knowledge of Jesus Christ and to strengthen the body of Christ worldwide. *Tony Evans Films* released its first feature-length film, *Kingdom Men Rising*, in April 2019, in over 800 theaters nationwide, in partnership with Lifeway Films. The second release, *Journey with Jesus*, is in partnership with RightNow Media and was released in theaters in November, 2021.

Resource Development

We are fostering lifelong learning partnerships with the people we serve by providing a variety of published materials. Dr. Evans has published more than 125 unique titles based on over 50 years of preaching, whether that is in booklet, book, or Bible study format. He also holds the honor of writing and publishing the first full-Bible commentary and study Bible by an African American, which released in 2019. This Bible sits in permanent display as a historic release in The Museum of the Bible in Washington, DC.

For more information and a complimentary copy of Dr. Evans's devotional newsletter, call (800) 800-3222, write TUA at P.O. Box 4000, Dallas, TX 75208, or visit online at www.tonyevans.org.

ABOUT THE AUTHOR

Dr. Tony Evans is one of the country's most respected leaders in evangelical circles. He is a pastor, bestselling author, and frequent speaker at Bible conferences and seminars throughout the nation.

Dr. Evans has served as the senior pastor of Oak Cliff Bible Fellowship for over forty years, witnessing it grow from ten people in 1976 to now over ten thousand congregants and over one hundred ministries.

He also serves as president of The Urban Alternative, a national ministry that seeks to restore hope and transform lives through the proclamation and application of the Word of God. His daily radio broadcast, *The Alternative with Dr. Tony Evans*, can be heard on over 1,400 radio outlets throughout the United States and in more than 130 countries.

Dr. Evans holds the honor of writing and publishing the first full-Bible commentary and study Bible by an African American. The study Bible and commentary went on to sell more than 225,000 copies in the first year.

He is the former chaplain for the Dallas Cowboys and the Dallas Mavericks.

Throughout his local church and national ministry, Dr. Evans has set in motion a kingdom-agenda philosophy of ministry that teaches God's comprehensive rule over every area of life as demonstrated through the individual, the family, the church, and society.

Dr. Evans was married to Lois, his wife and ministry partner of over fifty years, until Lois transitioned to glory in late 2019. They are the proud parents of four, grandparents of thirteen, and great-grandparents of three.